Medical Professionalism
Best Practices

Edited by
Richard L. Byyny, MD
Maxine A. Papadakis, MD
Douglas S. Paauw, MD

2015
Alpha Omega Alpha Honor Medical Society
Menlo Park, California

i

Dedicated to the members of Alpha Omega Alpha Honor Medical Society and the medical profession

Publication of this monograph was funded by a President's Grant from the Josiah Macy Jr. Foundation.

Medical Professionalism: Best Practices

Edited by Richard L. Byyny, MD; Maxine A. Papadakis, MD; Douglas S. Paauw, MD

© 2015, Alpha Omega Alpha Honor Medical Society

ISBN: 978-0-578-16071-9
eBook ISBN: 978-0-578-16072-6

Contributors

Richard L. Byyny, MD (AΩA, University of Southern California, 1964), is the Executive Director of Alpha Omega Alpha Honor Medical Society, and was previously Professor of Medicine at the University of Colorado School of Medicine. From 1997 through 2005, Dr. Byyny served as the Chancellor of the University of Colorado at Boulder. Contact Dr. Byyny at: Alpha Omega Alpha, 525 Middlefield Road, Suite 130, Menlo Park, California 94025. E-mail: r.byyny@alphaomegaalpha.org.

Anna Chang, MD (AΩA, St. Louis University, 2000), is Associate Professor of Medicine in the Division of Geriatrics, Department of Medicine, at the University of California, San Francisco, School of Medicine. Contact Dr. Chang at: University of California, San Francisco, School of Medicine, 3333 California Street, Laurel Heights, Room 380, San Francisco, California 94118. E-mail: anna.chang@ucsf.edu.

William O. Cooper, MD, MPH, is Cornelius Vanderbilt Professor and Associate Dean for Faculty Affairs at Vanderbilt University School of Medicine and the Director of the Vanderbilt Center for Patient and Professional Advocacy. Contact Dr. Cooper at: Center for Patient and Professional Advocacy, Vanderbilt University medical Center, 2135 Blakemore Avenue, Nashville, Tennessee 37212-3505. E-mail: william.cooper@vanderbilt.edu.

Richard M. Frankel, PhD, is Professor of Medicine and Geriatrics at the Indiana University School of Medicine, Director of the Mary Margaret Walther Program in Palliative Care Research and Education at the IU/Simon Cancer Center, and Associate Director of the VA HSR&D Center for Health Information and Communication. Contact Dr. Frankel at: Veterans Administration Medical Center, Room 11 HSR&D, 1481 West 10th Street, Indianapolis, Indiana 46202-2884. E-mail: rfrankel@iupui.edu.

Suely Grosseman, MD, PhD, is Professor of Pediatrics at the Federal University of Santa Catarina (Brazil). Contact Dr. Grosseman at: Universidade Federal de Santa Catarina—Campus Reitor João David Ferreira Lima Centro de Ciências da Saúde, Departamento de Pediatria Florianópolis, Santa Catarina, Brasil CEP: 88040-900. E-mail: sgrosseman@gmail.com.

Gerald B. Hickson, MD, is Assistant Vice Chancellor for Health Affairs and Senior Vice President of Quality, Safety and Risk Prevention at Vanderbilt University School of Medicine. Contact Dr. Hickson at: Quality and Patient Safety, 2135 Blakemore Avenue, Campus Zip 8627, Nashville, Tennessee 37212. E-mail: gerald.b.hickson@vanderbilt.edu.

Catherine R. Lucey, MD (AΩA, Northwestern University, 1980), is Professor of Medicine and Vice Dean for Medical Education at the

University of California, San Francisco, School of Medicine. Contact Dr. Lucey at: University of California, San Francisco, School of Medicine, Box 0410, 521 Parnassus Avenue, Clinic Sci Room 254, San Francisco, California 94143. E-mail: luceyc@medsch.ucsf.edu.

Dennis H. Novack, MD (AΩA, Drexel University, 2001), is Professor of Medicine and Associate Dean of Medical Education at Drexel University College of Medicine. He is a 2011 recipient of the AΩA Robert J. Glaser Distinguished Teacher Award. Contact Dr. Novack at: Drexel University College of Medicine, 2126 Fairmount Avenue, Philadelphia, Pennsylvania 19130. E-mail: dennis.novack@drexelmed.edu.

Douglas S. Paauw, MD (AΩA, University of Michigan, 1983), is Director, Medicine Student Programs, Professor of Medicine, and Rathmann Family Foundation Endowed Chair in Patient-Centered Clinical Education at the University of Washington School of Medicine. He is a 2001 recipient of the AΩA Robert J. Glaser Distinguished Teacher Award, President of the Board of Directors of Alpha Omega Alpha, and AΩA councilor at the University of Washington. Contact Dr. Paauw at: University of Washington School of Medicine, Department of Internal Medicine, Box 356420, 1959 NE Pacific Street, Seattle, Washington 98195-6420. E-mail: dpaauw@medicine.washington.edu.

Maxine Papadakis, MD (AΩA, University of California, San Francisco, 1993), is Professor of Medicine and Associate Dean for Students at the University of California, San Francisco, School of Medicine. She was member of the Board of Directors of Alpha Omega Alpha from 2005 through 2007. Contact Dr. Papadakis at: University of California, San Francisco, School of Medicine, 513 Parnassus Avenue, S-245, San Francisco, California 94143-0454. E-mail: papadakm@medsch.ucsf.edu.

Sheryl A. Pfeil, MD (AΩA, Ohio State University, 1984), is Associate Professor of Clinical Internal Medicine and Medical Director of the Clinical Skills Education and Assessment Center at Ohio State University College of Medicine. She is a member of the Board of Directors of Alpha Omega Alpha and the AΩA councilor at Ohio State. Contact Dr. Pfeil at: Ohio State University, Division of Gastroenterology, Hepatology and Nutrition, 395 W. 12th Avenue, Suite 200, Columbus, Ohio 43210. E-mail: sheryl.pfeil@osumc.edu.

Rebecca Saavedra, EdD, is Vice President of Strategic Management in the Office of the President, and Co-Chair of the UTMB Professionalism Committee. Contact Dr. Saavedra at: The University of Texas Medical Branch at Galveston, Office of the President Mail Route 0127, 301 University Boulevard, Galveston, Texas 77555-0127. E-mail: rsaavedr@utmb.edu.

Jo Shapiro, MD (AΩA, George Washington University, 1980), is

Associate Professor of Otolaryngology at Harvard Medical School and Director of the Center for Professionalism and Peer Support and Chief of the Division of Otolaryngology in the Department of Surgery at Brigham and Women's Hospital. Contact Dr. Shapiro at: Brigham and Women's Hospital, Division of Otolaryngology, 45 Francis Street, ASB-2, Boston, Massachusetts 02115. E-mail: jshapiro@partners.org.

George Thibault, MD (AΩA, Harvard Medical School, 1968), has served as the President of the Josiah Macy Jr. Foundation since 2008. He is the Daniel D. Federman Professor of Medicine and Medical Education, Emeritus, at Harvard Medical School. He was previously Vice President of Clinical Affairs at Partners Healthcare System in Boston and Director of the Academy at Harvard Medical School. Contact Dr. Thibault at: The Josiah Macy Jr. Foundation, 44 East 64th Street, New York, New York 10065. E-mail: info@macyfoundation.org.

Deborah Ziring, MD, is Assistant Professor in the Department of Medicine at Drexel University College of Medicine. Contact Dr. Ziring at: Drexel University College of Medicine, 2900 Queen Lane, Room 221, Philadelphia, Pennsylvania 19129. E-mail: deborah.ziring@drexelmed.edu.

Acknowledgments

Thanks to Dr. John A. Benson, Jr. (AΩA, Oregon Health & Science University, 1968), and Dr. Jack Coulehan (AΩA, University of Pittsburgh, 1969), who serve on AΩA's Professionalism Award Committee and on the editorial board of *The Pharos*, for their help in reviewing and improving this monograph.

We thank the Josiah Macy Jr. Foundation for its President's Grant, which funded the publication and distribution of this monograph.

Table of Contents

Preface
Medical Professionalism: Best Practices
Richard L. Byyny, MD

Professionalism in medicine has been a core value for Alpha Omega Alpha Honor Medical Society (AΩA) since the society's founding in 1902. Demonstrated professionalism is one of the criteria for election to membership in AΩA. In the Winter 2000 issue of AΩA's quarterly journal *The Pharos*, Executive Director Edward D. Harris, Jr., MD (1997–2010), wrote, "The profession of medicine is under siege. Our resistance must be professionalism." In 2009, AΩA established an annual Edward D. Harris Professionalism Award that encourages teaching faculty to create appropriate learning environments for professionalism, or new programs to ingrain professionalism in medical students and resident physicians. Since then, AΩA has made annual awards and continued its work to promote, understand, and support medical professionalism.

Because medical professionalism is a core value of the society, the board of directors of AΩA has discussed how the society can serve as a leader and a catalyst to improve medical professionalism. We wanted to better understand medical professionalism, professionalism issues, and learn about teaching and supporting research and scholarship related to medical professionalism, identifying methods of evaluating aspects of professionalism, and finding a leadership focus for AΩA in medical professionalism.

In 1914, U.S. Supreme Court Justice Louis Brandeis defined a profession:

First. A profession is an occupation for which the necessary preliminary training is intellectual in character, involving knowledge, and to some extent learning, as distinguished from mere skill.

Second. A profession is an occupation which is pursued largely for others and not merely for one's self.

Third. It is an occupation in which the amount of financial return is not the accepted measure of success.

Our efforts in medical professionalism are a work in progress. As physicians, we are gradually and continually learning about medical professionalism and how to maintain and improve a standard of physician behavior. We need to remember that we call our work "the practice of medicine" because we are always practicing our profession to learn and improve. We also need to remember that our goal is not perfection, but continuous learning, improvement, and focusing on what is best for the patient. We recognize medical professionalism as an important issue for doctors and society that must be taught and then practiced in the interests of both patients and our profession.

We have begun to make progress, but the challenges are huge. Since AΩA developed the Edward D. Harris Professionalism Award a few years ago as our society's contribution to promote professionalism in medicine, we have made awards for some interesting projects but haven't had a clear focus about AΩA's leadership role and how the society's programs and projects can make a positive difference in medical professionalism—is it in curriculum reform, remediation, or some other important step toward the future?

We are committed to focusing our efforts at AΩA to define our role in the development of professionalism in medicine. Many AΩA members are leaders in medicine. We recognize that developing effective leadership in medicine must continue to be grounded in professional values. It is clear that the combination of leadership and professionalism can have a synergistic and positive impact on our members and profession.

To learn more about medical professionalism, we sponsored and hosted an AΩA Think Tank Meeting on Medical Professionalism in July 2011. We brought together experts in medical professionalism to review and discuss the status of and challenges in the field. That meeting was based on the assumption that the last twenty years have seen good progress in defining professionalism and in devising charters, curricula, assessment strategies, and accreditation criteria. However, participants recognized that there has been insufficient evidence to inform best practices in medical professionalism. This is especially true for interventions and remediation strategies for those who demonstrate lapses in professionalism and professional behaviors. The meeting resulted in the publication in *Academic Medicine* of "Perspective: The Education Community Must Develop Best Practices Informed by Evidence-based Research to Remediate Lapses of Professionalism."[1] The meeting participants identified two issues as very important to medical professionalism:

1. How can we use existing data on professionalism remediation?

2. What new evidence is needed to advance approaches to remediation of unprofessional performance?

Participants also recommended that the education community focus on interventions and remediation by performing studies about improving medical professionalism when lapses occur, identifying best evidence-based remediation practices, widely disseminating those practices, and moving over time from a best-practice approach to remediation (which does not yet exist) to a best-evidence model.

This monograph, *Medical Professionalism: Best Practices*, is the result of a subsequent AΩA sponsored meeting, Best Practices in Medical Professionalism, which had two themes:

1. Use of systems to enhance professionalism
2. Best practices for the remediation of lapses in professionalism

The authors in this monograph presented some of the identified best practices, followed by discussion, questions, and debate. We thank the Josiah Macy Jr. Foundation for its President's Grant, which funds the publication and distribution of this monograph. The Foundation's president, Dr. George E. Thibault, participated in our meeting and has written the concluding chapter.

The co-chairs of the meeting, co-editors of this monograph, and authors of two chapters are Dr. Maxine Papadakis and Dr. Douglas S. Paauw.

AΩA and medical professionalism

Medicine is based on a covenant of trust, a contract we in medicine have with patients and society. Medical professionalism stands on the foundation of trust to create an interlocking structure among physicians, patients, and society that determines medicine's values and responsibilities in the care of the patient and improving public health. AΩA supports and advocates for medical professionalism as a core value of the society.

The founding of AΩA is interesting and important to medical professionalism. William Root and other medical students at the College of Physicians and Surgeons of Chicago founded AΩA in 1902, before the Abraham Flexner report and the subsequent transformation of medical education. Root and likeminded fellow students were shocked by the lack of interest in high achievement, especially high academic achievement, by the faculty and their fellow students. They found the behavior of students and faculty to be boorish and clearly lacking in professional values. They decided to establish a medical honor society based on the model of Phi Beta Kappa. They wrote, "The mission of AΩA is to encourage high ideals of thought and action in schools of medicine and to promote that which is the highest in professional practice." They defined the duties of AΩA members: "to foster the scientific and philosophical features of the medical profession and of the public, to cultivate social mindedness as well as an individualistic attitude toward responsibilities, to show respect for colleagues and especially for elders and teachers, to foster research, and in all ways to strive to ennoble the profession of medicine and advance it in public opinion. It is equally a duty to avoid what is unworthy, including the commercial spirit and all practices injurious to the welfare of patients, the public or the profession." They established the AΩA motto: "Be worthy to serve the suffering." Since its founding, AΩA has celebrated, advocated, and supported the principles of high academic achievement, leadership, demonstrated professionalism, service, research and scholarship, and teaching in medicine. Election to membership in AΩA is based on outstanding scholarly achievement and these core professional values.[2]

AΩA expanded rapidly throughout the early twentieth century and continues to expand in the twenty-first century. There are now 126 AΩA chapters in medical schools, with more than 150,000 members. Member dues provide nearly three-quarters of a million dollars to support the following AΩA programs and awards each year: the Robert J. Glaser Distinguished Teaching Awards, the Carolyn Kuckein Medical Student Research Fellowships, AΩA Visiting Professorships at medical schools, Medical Student Service Leadership Project Awards, Postgraduate Awards, Volunteer Clinical Faculty Awards, Administrative Recognition Awards, Student Essay Awards, the *Pharos* Poetry Competition, three AΩA Fellow in Leadership Awards, and the Edward D. Harris Professionalism Award. The society's quarterly journal, *The Pharos*, publishes essays at the intersection of medicine and the humanities, as well as news about activities, awards, and programs.

The history of medical professionalism

The first oath for medical ethics was apparently written as the Code of Hammurabi in 2000 BC. Hippocrates and Maimonides subsequently developed oaths codifying the practice of medicine as the sacred trust of the physician to protect and care for the patient and a set of values for physicians appropriate for their times.[3,4] Both emphasized teaching and learning, and the primacy of benefiting the sick according to one's ability and judgment while adhering to high principles and ideals. These oaths were also a form of social contract that partially codified what patients and society should expect from the physician.

The physician Scribonius apparently coined the word "profession" in 47 AD. He referred to the profession as a commitment to compassion, benevolence, and clemency in the relief of suffering, and emphasized humanitarian values.[5] While patients and societies and the concept of medical professionalism have changed over time, many of the professional values in medicine are timeless. To paraphrase Sir William Osler: "The practice of medicine is an art; a calling, not a business; a calling in which your heart will be exercised equally with your head; a calling which extracts from you at every turn self-sacrifice, devotion, love and tenderness to your fellow man." He also wrote, "No doubt medicine is a science, but it is a science of uncertainty and an art of probability."[6]

The science of medicine has progressed dramatically in the last hundred years. Up until the mid-1900s, doctors could diagnose some illnesses based on the patient's history, but they had few diagnostic tests or effective therapies. Thus one of the special roles of doctors—the art of medicine—was to relieve patients' suffering. Scientific and technical advances brought more effective treatments, which paradoxically led many doctors to become less capable of compassionately caring for the suffering patient.

During the last fifty years, social changes have altered the relationship of the doctor and patient. In what is sometimes referred to as the corporate transformation of health care, many components of medicine have become businesses that do not put the patient first and dismiss the special relationship between patients and their doctors. At the same time, the profession of medicine has not responded as effectively as it should have to protect the primacy of the care of the patient. We believe that serving as a physician and practicing medicine must be based on core professional beliefs and values, and that those entering and practicing our profession must understand the values of medical professionalism and learn and demonstrate the aptitude and commitment to behave professionally. Physicians work primarily in the service to others and our success is measured in human terms, by how well we benefit those under our care, not necessarily in financial returns. We are evaluated and respected because of what we actually do and how we meet our responsibilities. A physician's work is compassionate and includes a commitment to service, altruism, and advocacy. Our profession of medicine is self-directed and therefore self-regulating. The privilege of self-regulation is granted to us by patients and society when we prove ourselves worthy of their trust by meeting our professional responsibilities to them.

Professionalism is a required core competency for physicians. A few decades ago, medical professionalism became an important issue. Many researchers concluded that an integrated patient-centered approach was needed, one that included both the science and the art of medicine. While a disease framework is required to reach a diagnosis and select appropriate therapy, the illness framework in which the patient's unique and personal experience with suffering, including individual worries, concerns, feelings, and beliefs, is equally important. Some recognized that what Francis W. Peabody wrote earlier was both straightforward and profoundly important: "One of the essential qualities of the clinician is interest in humanity, for the secret of the care of the patient is in caring for the patient."[7]

Medical professionalism today

In dissecting medical professionalism to better understand the concept and determine how to address issues of concern both to the profession and society, most researchers have concluded that the profound and rapid advances in medical knowledge, technology, specialized skills, and expertise have inadvertently resulted in a loss of our professional core values. Many writers and professional organizations have proposed a renewed commitment to restore professionalism to the core of what doctors do. It seems self-evident that we should practice medicine based on core professional beliefs and values. In my opinion, this relates first and foremost to the doctor-patient relationship. It starts with physicians understanding their obligations and commitments to serve and care for people, especially the suffering. Physicians must put patients first and subordinate their own interests to those of others. They should also adhere to high ethical and moral standards and a set of medical professional values. These values start with the precept of "Do no harm." They include a simple code of conduct that explicitly states: no lying, no stealing, no cheating, nor tolerance for those who do. I also believe that the Golden Rule, or ethic of reciprocity, common to many cultures throughout the world—"one should treat others as one would like others to treat oneself"—should be the ethical code or moral basis for how we treat each other.

Professional organizations and leaders in medicine have recently defined the fundamental principles of medical professionalism. CanMEDS 2000 stated it well: "Physicians should deliver the highest quality of care with integrity, honesty, and compassion and should be committed to the health and well-being of individuals and society through ethical practice, professionally led regulation, and high personal standards of behaviour."

The American College of Physicians and the American Board of Internal Medicine have developed a physician charter with three fundamental principles:

1. The primacy of patient welfare or dedication to serving the interest of the patient, and the importance of altruism and trust

2. Patient autonomy, including honesty and respect for the patients to make decisions about their care

3. Social justice, to eliminate discrimination in health care for any reason.[8]

Professional organizations have also developed a set of professional responsibilities:

- Professional competence
- Honesty with patients
- Patient confidentiality
- Maintaining appropriate relations with patients
- Improving quality of care
- Improving access to care
- Just distribution of finite resources
- Scientific knowledge
- Maintaining trust by managing conflicts of interest

- Professional responsibility

I also believe explicit rules and values are important in medicine and I have taken the liberty to rephrase some and add others in the following table.[1] Learning requires a clear, straightforward set of expectations combined with learning opportunities, reflection, evaluation, and feedback, and these principles may provide an important basis for physician learning.

Professionalism in Medicine	
Responsibilities to patients	
The care of your patient is your first concern	Care for patients in an ethical, responsible, reliable, and respectful manner
Do no harm	Respect patients' dignity, privacy, and confidentiality
No lying, stealing, or cheating, nor tolerance for those who do	Respect patients' rights to make decisions about their care
Commit to professional competence and lifelong learning	Communicate effectively and listen to patients with understanding and respect for their views
Accept professional and personal responsibility for the care of patients	Be honest and trustworthy and keep your word with patients
Use your knowledge and skills in the best interest of the patient	Maintain appropriate relations with your patients
Treat every patient humanely, with benevolence, compassion, empathy, and consideration	Reflect frequently on your care of patients, including your values and behaviors
Social responsibilities and advocacy	
Commit and advocate to improve quality of care and access to care	Respect and work with colleagues and other health professionals to best serve the patients' needs
Commit and advocate for a just distribution of finite resources	Commit to maintaining trust by managing conflicts of interest

While I hope that most physicians understand, practice, and teach with professionalism and its core values, the literature indicates that unprofessional behaviors are common. This raises the question: Can you teach professional behaviors to students and physicians? Although medical schools would like to select students who already have professional values and ethics, they lack reliable tools to find those candidates and so primarily rely on academic performance for admission.

Medical schools transmit knowledge, teach skills, and try to embed the values of the medical profession. During this curriculum and learning process do students learn to put the needs of patients first? Most of the data indicate that students begin with a sense of altruism, values, and open-mindedness, but they learn to focus on what is tested to pass examinations. They observe self-interest, a focus on income, and nonprofessional behaviors by their seniors in our profession and unfortunately grow progressively more cynical and less professional, especially once they get to clinical experiences. This is worsened by the lack of moral and professional values in the business and political components of medicine that often disregard the patient and the patient's needs and interests.

Although most schools have curricula related to professional values, what students learn and retain is from what is called the "hidden curriculum"—the day-to-day experiences of students working in the clinical environment while watching, listening, and emulating resident and physician behaviors. It is not a good story. Fortunately, some schools and teaching hospitals have implemented effective interventions to improve medical professionalism, and some have attempted to develop methods of evaluating aspects of professionalism. Having a few courses, however, does not seem to make a difference in learning professionalism and professional behaviors. The most effective programs, so far, lead by changing the institutional culture and environment to respect and reward professional behavior, while at the same time exposing and working to change the negative impact of the "hidden curriculum." Many of these interventions are top-down and bottom-up institutional changes that focus on faculty, house staff, students, and staff members, and have shown promising reports of changes in professionalism.

We shouldn't presume that professional core values in medicine are intuitively apparent. I recognize there is continuing debate about the importance and value of a physician's "oath" or "solemn promise," but I believe we must have clear professional expectations that are explicit for all physicians and a commitment from physicians to respect and uphold a code of professional values and behaviors. In my opinion, these include the commitment to:

- Adhere to high ethical and moral standards: do right, avoid wrong, and do no harm.
- Subordinate your own interests to those of your patients.
- Avoid business, financial, and organizational conflicts of interest.
- Honor the social contract you have undertaken with patients and communities.

• Understand the non-biologic determinants of poor health and the economic, psychological, social, and cultural factors that contribute to health and illness.

• Care for patients who are unable to pay, and advocate for the medically underserved.

• Be accountable, both ethically and financially.

• Be thoughtful, compassionate, and collegial.

• Continue to learn, increase your competence, and strive for excellence.

• Work to advance the field of medicine, and share knowledge for the benefit of others.

• Reflect dispassionately on your own actions, behaviors, and decisions to improve your knowledge, skills, judgment, decision-making, accountability, and professionalism.[9]

The chapters in this monograph, *Medical Professionalism: Best Practices*, present their authors' experiences both in building cultures of medical professionalism and dealing with lapses in professionalism. We hope that it will support medical schools, professional organizations, practitioners, and all involved in health care in their very important work on professionalism in medicine.

Bibliography and references

1. Papadakis MA, Paauw DS, Hafferty FW, et al. Perspective: The education community must develop best practices informed by evidence-based research to remediate lapses of professionalism. Acad Med 2012; 87: 1694–98.

2. Byyny RL. AΩA and professionalism in medicine. The Pharos Summer 2011; 74: 1–3.

3. Edelstein L. The Hippocratic Oath: Text, Translation and Interpretation. Baltimore (MD): Johns Hopkins University Press; 1943.

4. Tan SY, Yeow ME. Moses Maimonides (1135–1204): Rabbi, philosopher, physician. Singapore Med J 2002; 43: 551–53.

5. Hamilton JS. Scribonius Largus on the medical profession. Bull Hist Med 1986; 60:209–16.

6. Bliss M. William Osler: A Life in Medicine. New York: Oxford University Press; 2007.

7. Oglesby P. The Caring Physician: The Life of Dr. Francis W. Peabody. Cambridge (MA): Harvard University Press; 1991.

8. ABIM Foundation, American Board of Internal Medicine; ACP-ASIM Foundation, American College of Physicians-American Society of Internal Medicine; European Federation of Internal Medicine. Medical professionalism in the new millennium: a physician charter. Ann Intern Med 2002; 136: 243–46.

9. Byyny RL. AΩA and professionalism in medicine—continued. The Pharos

Introduction

Chapter 1

Introduction

Maxine A. Papadakis, MD

The longstanding commitment to enhancing professionalism by the Alpha Omega Alpha Honor Medical Society (AΩA) and the Josiah Macy Jr. Foundation is remarkable. Their recent commitment to highlighting the need to focus on remediation strategies to address lapses in professional behavior is farsighted and welcome in the educational community. Many tools have been developed to assess professional behavior, but as was pointed out in the 2011 AΩA Think Tank on lapses in professionalism,[1] assessment has limited value unless it leads to improvement. What is known about remediation for lapses of professional behavior in medical students? Hauer et al. reviewed the published outcome data on remediation efforts in a 2009 paper in *Academic Medicine*.[2] She and her colleagues found that many of the published studies lacked the robust scientific outcomes that learners and medical educators deserve. The conclusion from the Hauer paper was that there was an urgent need from multi-institutional outcomes-based research on strategies for remediation.

This monograph addresses professional behaviors and organizational structures as they impact professionalism. Here we present a framework for the papers that follow. The first group of papers addresses systems and organizational structures that influence the professionalism of every member of a community, but lapses by medical students get particular attention. In order to do so, studies about lapses of the professional behavior of faculty and practicing physicians are extrapolated to lapses in medical students. The next set of papers addresses interventions directed at an individual learner.

Definitions of professionalism based on lists of measureable professional behaviors are functional for teaching, assessment, and certification. In several ways, though, there is a risk that the list-based definitions will obscure the foundational purpose of professionalism, a view supported by many broad definitions of professionalism, including a recent one written for the American Board of Medical Specialties.[3] The broader understanding of professionalism extends beyond definitions and behaviors. Defining professionalism as a list of personal attributes suggests that the operationalization of professionalism is only at the level of the individual, which may deflect attention from the essential organizational and systems structures that underline professionalism. Professionalism transcends the list of desirable values and behaviors; it is the belief system, the reason for creating the lists and acting in accordance with them.[3] Lesser and colleagues have pointed out the fallacy in the belief that medical educators can come up with an exhaustive list of the professional behaviors that learners will need across the continuum of their education.[4] Rather, these authors offer a broader perspective of professionalism by calling for the need to educate learners to recognize and navigate conflicts in professionalism. This broader perspective of professionalism will help learners when we cannot articulate what those behaviors are.

While respecting the broader perspective that professionalism is a belief system that transcends behaviors, there remains a compelling need for the delineation of best practices to address lapses in professional behavior while we await evidence from interventional studies. "Best practices" at this time means "best consensus opinions" based on the experience and expertise of medical education faculty, particularly those from the student affairs arena. Consensus expert opinion is available and does not need to wait for the truly "best practices" based on evidence with documented outcomes. Best consensus opinions could be gathered to answer questions such as what should be the academic consequences for a third-year medical student who at the end of a required clerkship demonstrates mastery in fund of knowledge and clinical problem-solving skills, but not professionalism. Since the competency of professionalism is one of the six core Accredited Council of Medical Education (ACME) competencies, should the medical student repeat the clerkship? If the medical student is to repeat the clerkship, should there be an intervention to remediate the student's deficiency in the competency of professionalism? Alternatively, since the medical student is being given another chance to learn skills in professionalism by observing and modeling behaviors when repeating the clerkship, is the experience gained from repeating the clerkship adequate remediation? If the student is not to repeat the clerkship (the assumption, therefore, is that the student passed the rotation), what remediation plans should be put in place to help the student? What should be the outcome measures?

Medical schools can use such best practices to fulfill their responsibility to graduate physicians who leave medical school with the school's confidence that the physician will act professionally. Best practices will reflect a consensus of the education community about what is the right thing to do and how much is reasonable for schools to do to fulfill their obligation to create the educational environment in which learners excel. Best practices can help clarify the boundary between the school's obligations and the individual learner's obligation to meet the competency of professionalism. Best practices can help answer the question of whether a medical school has done enough to help a learner who is having lapses in professional behavior. Does the medical school have the right resources and the right systems in place to help the learner? Consensus about best practices will help medical schools answer the tough question of whether a learner should be allowed to continue in medical school or when it is time for the learner to leave because the educational community has come together and defined what are reasonable resources to help the learner.

The literature provides information about which professional behaviors are core and should be on lists of measurable professional behaviors for teaching, assessment, and certification. The choice to include these behaviors on lists, however, is based on the premise that these behaviors can be accurately and validly assessed. How do American medical schools assess professionalism? From a survey published in 2011,[5] professionalism is assessed by several modalities, but what links them together is direct observation. Direct observation is critical for the assessment of professionalism; it is not as critical for the assessment of fund of knowledge, for which more quantitative, multiple choice, and even essay testing formats are effective. A further discussion of assessment instruments is beyond the scope of this paper, but several tools to assess professional behavior have been developed and studied, including the Assessment of Professional Behaviors Program by the National Board of Medical Examiners (https://www.mededportal.org/publication/9902), the Professionalism Mini-evaluation Exercise,[6] the Conscientiousness Index,[7] and the physicianship forms from UCSF.[8,9]

The behaviors that comprise professionalism can be organized around four areas, which are: (1) responsibility; (2) capacity for self-improvement; (3) relationship with patients; and (4) relationship with the health care team and the environment, including systems and organizations. A 2005 study from UCSF, Jefferson Medical College, and University of Michigan Medical School linked unprofessional behavior during medical school with subsequent disciplinary action by state medical boards.[9] The presence of unprofessional behavior had the highest attributable risk (twenty-six percent) for subsequent disciplinary action of the measured predictor variables. That study described associations that were epidemiologic; the associations could not be extrapolated to an individual learner because of the limitations in sensitivity, specificity, and predictive value of the variables. The study did provide insights, however, about particular behaviors that were associated with subsequent disciplinary actions. Medical students who displayed a pattern of irresponsibility while in medical school were nearly nine times more likely to be subsequently disciplined by a medical licensing board; board actions could occur even decades later. Finding an odds ratio as high as nine in that retrospective study, while taking into account the limitations of the research design, is likely a conservative estimate of the risk and the importance of this behavior. Nine times a rare outcome, nonetheless, remains rare since less than a percent or so of physicians are disciplined by state licensing boards.

The behavior of irresponsibility includes unreliable attendance at clinic, problematic notification about missed attendance, not following up on activities related to patient care, being late or absent for assigned activities, and being unreliable. An example of an irresponsible student is one who repeatedly shows up late for didactic and small group sessions, as well as the start of a call day. The student has an imprecise excuse for being late; his peers are aware of the tardiness. Such learners can be taught that being responsible is an expectation of their professional development and that being irresponsible has risk for subsequent disciplinary actions. Behaviors in the domain of responsibility are measurable. What is unknown is the outcome of learners who display a pattern of irresponsibility and then receive remediation. Have these learners learned to stay under the radar screen or have they accepted the belief system of professionalism, with the ability to recognize and navigate challenges in professionalism?

The second behavior is diminished capacity for self-improvement, such as failure to accept or incorporate constructive criticism. This behavior includes interactions described as brusque, hostile, argumentative, or negative. A poor attitude, arrogance, over-confidence, or overly sensitive are additional descriptors. An example of such a student is one who is perceived as being demanding and insensitive to the needs of other students; the student often interrupts fellow students during their presentations. Nurses note that the student is arrogant. The staff notes that the student complains about the clinic schedule and requests changes to assignments. The student is vocal about the shortcomings of the school's evaluation system.

The third behavior centers around impaired relationship with patients, failure to establish rapport, and insensitivity to patients' needs. The fourth behavior concerns relationship with the health care environment, such as not being respectful to members of the health care team, and creating a hostile educational environment. The literature is replete with studies showing the importance of the medical team's dynamics for patient safety. The behaviors of testing irregularity and falsification of patient data are included here. Likely there is uniform consensus that falsification of patient data is unacceptable. What is unknown, however, is whether all testing irregularities should be of similar concern. If a student seated near another student copies an answer from a multiple choice test, is that as worrisome as someone who cheats on a licensing examination?

In addition to the four behaviors, one needs to pay attention to the pattern of lapses of professionalism within each behavior. An isolated lapse can be just that, isolated; the individual may be displaying poor coping skill for a compelling life event such as a flare in a health problem or a divorce. A pattern of lapses likely foreshadows later problems with disciplinary actions.[9]

Another consideration is when a lapse of professional behavior occurs. Are the implications the same for professionalism when a second-year medical student creates a hostile learning environment in a small group setting as when an attending physician creates a hostile learning environment for residents? Would the attending physician not have created a hostile learning environment if the operating room ran more efficiently? What are the accountability dynamics between inefficient systems and the individual physician?

The severity of the lapses is also important. Learners must be given the opportunity and skills to develop professionally, which include navigating challenges to professionalism and maturing over time, just as learners gain and improve their skills in fund of knowledge and clinical care. Minor lapses in professional behavior should be considered part of the developmental spectrum as the learner develops professional identify. Consideration about lapses in professional behavior must also take into account whether the learner is on a trajectory of improvement. Another context for lapses in professionalism may be when there is a change in the environment. Every time a student rotates onto a new clerkship, she becomes anxious, argumentative, and hostile. As she feels safer, her behavior improves. But the pattern does not improve as she repeats the cycle every time she rotates into a new setting.

The papers that follow explore professionalism from the lens of systems, the learner, and the patient.

References

1. Papadakis MA, Paauw DS, Hafferty FW, et al. Perspective: The education community must develop best practices informed by evidence-based research to remediate lapses of professionalism. Acad Med 2012; 87: 1694–98.

2. Hauer KE, Ciccone A, Henzel TR, et al. Remediation of the deficiencies of physicians across the continuum from medical school to practice: A thematic review of the literature. Acad Med 2009; 84: 1822–32.

3. Wynia MK, Papadakis MA, Sullivan WM, Hafferty FW. More than a list of values and desired behaviors: A foundational understanding of medical professionalism. Acad Med 2014; 89: 712–14.

4. Lesser CS, Lucey CR, Egener B, et al. A behavioral and systems view of professionalism. JAMA 2010; 304: 2732–37.

5. Barzansky B, Etzel SI. Medical schools in the United States, 2011–2012. JAMA 2012; 308: 2257–63.

6. Cruess R, McIlroy JH, Cruess S, et al. The Professionalism Mini-evaluation

Exercise: A preliminary investigation. Acad Med 2006; 81 (10 Suppl): S74–78.

7. McLachlan JC, Finn G, Macnaughton J. The conscientiousness index: A novel tool to explore students' professionalism. Acad Med 2009; 84: 559–65.

8. Papadakis MA, Hodgson CS, Teherani A, Kohatsu ND. Unprofessional behavior in medical school is associated with subsequent disciplinary action by a state medical board. Acad Med 2004; 79: 244–49.

9. Papadakis MA, Teherani A, Banach MA, et al. Disciplinary action by medical boards and prior behavior in medical school. N Engl J Med 2005; 353: 2673–82.

Chapter 2
The Problem with Professionalism
Catherine R. Lucey, MD

Although we may disagree with the size or the cause of the problem, many educators, practitioners, leaders, and unfortunately patients would agree that the medical profession currently has a problem with professionalism. All too often we have seen headline stories about physicians engaged in behavior that is not only unprofessional but criminal: murder, pedophilia, and financial fraud. While these are horrific, the profession generally has no difficulty in responding quickly to sanction or remove a physician who has engaged in these types of behaviors.

Unfortunately, these unusual circumstances represent the tip of the iceberg of professionalism problems. Our commitment to professionalism as a community is more often damaged by behaviors that can be seen daily in every care arena. Examples include overtly disruptive behaviors such as abuse of power manifested by failure to comply with evidence-based safety practices, and intimidation of others by yelling, profanity, and threats of physical violence. Also common are covertly disruptive behaviors such as failing to answer pages or complete essential paperwork on time. Even more common are daily incivilities: sarcastic comments on rounds about patients, specialty bashing, and snarky comments about learners. Perhaps most threatening to a culture of professionalism is our collective tolerance to these behaviors: many articles document the failure of physicians to step in and correct unprofessional behavior despite a commitment to professional self-regulation.

The causes of our problem with professionalism are complex and controversial

Many have hypothesized that the problem with professionalism is a result of changes in the generational commitment to professionalism as a result of the ACGME-mandated work hours restrictions, enacted across the country at the beginning of the twenty-first century. But in reality, concerns about the state of medical professionalism, as reflected in the exponential growth of peer-reviewed literature on this topic, began in the early 1980s.[1] This occurred in parallel with a number of significant events that disrupted the way that physicians related to each other, their patients, the health care systems in which they worked, and the learners they taught.

In the mid 1980s, the shift from pure fee-for-service reimbursement to a strategy based on diagnosis-related groups (DRG) dramatically shortened the number of days that patients spent in the hospital and increased the pressure on physicians to rapidly admit and discharge patients. The tragic death of Libby Zion ushered in an era in which the length of time residents spent in the hospital was dramatically curtailed. In the mid 1990s, fraudulent billing by some physicians led to the implementation of Physicians at Teaching Hospitals (PATH) regulations that changed the work flow of teaching hospital rounds. Teams could no longer share the work of documentation, and time for teaching decreased. In the late 1990s, the Balanced Budget Act plunged many academic medical centers into the red overnight and an era of high-volume-throughput medicine began. This further shortened already abbreviated hospital stays, making the development of relationships between residents and their hospital-ized patients more difficult. The Institute of Medicine reports on medical errors in 1999 and quality in 2002 publicized the difficulty of providing consistently high quality safe patient care. The move to shorten residency work hours across the country and in all disciplines clearly has impacted the ways in which we work and how learners view their roles, but this was only the most recent of a long line of challenges to professionalism.

Different types of problems require different types of solutions

A problem exists when there is a gap between the realities we experi-ence and the ideals to which we aspire. In the world of problem solving, there are two types of problems: technical and complex adaptive prob-lems.[2,3] Technical problems are easy to recognize and define. All who ex-perience them agree on the nature of the problem and the characteristics of the desired state. Technical problems either exist in isolation or are relatively unaffected by changes in the environment. Solutions to techni-cal problems are well established, can be found in a book on a shelf or an article on the Internet, and can be outsourced. Once fixed, a technical problem tends to stay fixed. Classic technical problems are fixing a flat tire or a dripping water faucet.

In contrast, complex adaptive problems are characterized by contro-versy and volatility. They arise insidiously out of seemingly stable envi-ronments. People will disagree about the extent, nature, or cause of the complex adaptive problem and often they will disagree on the character-istics of the ideal state. Complex adaptive problems are highly influenced by the environments in which they exist and thus are always changing. The controversial and complex nature of these problems means that no "off-the-shelf" solution is possible: the people who experience the prob-lem must work and learn together to address the problem using multiple lenses. Because they are highly susceptible to environmental influences, complex adaptive problems are almost never permanently solved; they are merely managed as well as they can be within their existing contexts. They require continuous tending. Classic complex problems include poverty, drug addiction, underperforming schools, and teenage pregnancy.

The clues to the nature of the problem of professionalism are evident in the published literature and in presentations at national meetings. Articles have carefully explored beliefs about professionalism, searched for causes of deteriorating culture of professionalism, and called for a renewed commitment to professionalism. Debates are heard throughout academic medical center: Is professionalism worse than it has been in the past? Is it a pervasive problem or one that is isolated to a few bad actors? Is this a problem with the new generation of physicians or the most seasoned generations? We might similarly disagree on the future ideal: is altruism an outdated idea in the era of regulated work hours?

Sustaining professionalism is a complex adaptive problem

It is clear from these questions that the problem of sustaining professionalism meets all the criteria of a complex adaptive problem. Despite this, the medical profession has approached the problem as a technical one: seeking the single true cause and best solution even though the complexity of the problem mandates a different approach. The reliance on technical approaches stems from a commonly held assumption that professionalism is a dichotomous virtue—either present or absent in any given individual. The technical approach that follows this perspective is illustrated as a series of sequenced strategies, largely concentrated in the medical education environment. The strategies: recruit the right people, teach them the rules of professionalism, expose them to role models who skillfully apply those rules in the clinical environment, and then reward them with an MD degree and release them into the public. During this process, assess them carefully and be ready to impose sanctions or remove them from the profession if they commit a professionalism lapse. There is some data to suggest that the medical education environment does have a role as a gatekeeper for professionalism. In a seminal article in the *New England Journal of Medicine*, Papadakis and colleagues documented that physicians who were sanctioned by medical boards for unprofessional behavior were more likely to have been the recipients of more than one professionalism complaint during their medical school careers.[4]

Our current solutions are insufficient or ineffective

But if one reviews the literature that evaluates the success of interventions aligned with this approach, the results are disappointing. The problem with optimizing recruitment as a strategy for enhancing professionalism should be evident. Little data exists at the time of admission to medical school that could or should predict an individual's ability to live the values of professionalism in the clinical environment.[5,6] Scores on standardized exams, whether they test knowledge of the life and physical sciences or the social and behavioral sciences, may indicate whether the individual has mastered knowledge that would help an individual understand a particular challenge, but not whether he or she then will act in a desired fashion when confronted with that challenge. Interview questions and essays may uncover whether a potential student can articulate the values of professionalism and identify those who aspire to live those values. However, very few applicants to medical school have had the opportunity to test their ability to live those values in the stressful environment of health care.

The idea that professionalism can be taught as a series of rules has also proved to be problematic. On the surface, it is attractive to translate the abstract constructs of professionalism (altruism, respect, confidentiality, integrity, professional self regulation) into desired rules and behaviors. Campbell's survey of over 1,000 internists demonstrated that while the vast majority of physicians surveyed agreed with the tenets of professionalism, many were aware of instances in which they themselves or their colleagues did not live up to those values.[7] Huddle noted that this disconnect between intent and behavior was such a common situation that the ancient Greeks had a specific word for it: *akrasia*, meaning that the spirit was willing but the flesh was weak.[8]

The story becomes more complex still when we rely on the teaching of rules to educate and assess professionalism. In a series of elegant experiments, Ginsberg and colleagues concluded that the rules of professionalism are not static and universal, but highly contextual.[9] Additionally, faculty physicians provided with several exemplar cases of professionalism challenges were both externally and internally inconsistent in their decisions about what was the professional thing to do and why.[10] In one scenario, faculty were asked to identify the right response of a medical student who, after being instructed by his faculty physician not to inform a patient of a new diagnosis, is specifically asked by the patient to disclose the diagnosis. Some faculty stated emphatically that the student should reveal the diagnosis because the student should never lie; others said that the student should lie to the patient under these circumstances. Furthermore, those physicians who maintained that students should never lie to a patient subsequently suggested that there were cases in which the right response might be to lie. This work suggests that professional responses to complex situations are nuanced and not reducible to a core set of rules or commandments. In light of the variability of "correct responses" by different faculty, it also raises the concerns about the validity and reliability of assessing professionalism based on the response to isolated incidents.

Given the poor performance of rules as a mechanism for teaching, one might conclude that professionalism education must rely upon assigning students to role models who have successfully learned to deal with the ambiguity of professionalism challenges and who can articulate why a specific response is appropriate in a given situation. Unfortunately, the literature on the impact of role models in teaching professionalism is also disappointing. Hafferty coined the term "the hidden curriculum," describing the frequent disconnect between the lessons that are explicitly taught in the classroom and those that are modeled, learned, and rewarded in the clinical environment.[11] The inability of all role models, particularly those that appear to be otherwise professionally successful, to apply the lofty professionalism values in the clinical arena contributes to cynicism in trainees that may progress during training.[12]

If recruitment strategies are unreliable, rules are ambiguous and contextual, and role modeling by professionals is inconsistent, then perhaps the solution to the problem of professionalism must default to aggressive assessment and removal of those who exhibit unprofessional behaviors. Unfortunately, this also is an incomplete solution to the problem. As noted previously, faculty disagree about what the "right" behavior is in given professionalism challenges. This means that whether a behavior exhibited by a learner is deemed unprofessional depends on who is doing the observation: hardly a strong basis on which to take action. Furthermore, those with the power or authority to take corrective action may not be present when learners are engaging in acts of unprofessional behavior. Finally, literature exists that documents that faculty who do witness unprofessional behavior may be reluctant to address that behavior in any way.[13] Mizrahi was particularly dismayed by what he described as a set of maladaptive behaviors that physicians engaged in rather than confront a colleague who had made an error. He described these as denial ("It wasn't unprofessional"), discounting ("It was unprofessional but it was warranted"), or distancing ("It was unprofessional but let's just move on").[14] Faculty or colleagues may also fail to correct a professionalism lapse because they lack confidence in their ability to intervene successfully or they may be concerned that a report to a higher authority will result in sanctions that are disproportionate to the episode that they witnessed.

Evaluating professionalism lapses as a form of medical error

When problems cannot be solved with conventional approaches, new learning is required. In considering common professionalism lapses, we recognized that there are similarities between professionalism lapses and medical errors. Like medical errors, professionalism lapses are more common than we might think. They occur in predictable circumstances: when individuals are stressed, the situations are highly charged, and controversy is present. Professionalism lapses range in severity from largely invisible (for example, the faculty member who claims CME credit for a lecture he didn't attend) to potentially fatal (the resident who leaves the hospital without checking on a post-procedure chest X-ray). As is the case with medical errors, those whom we otherwise consider to be good physicians commit occasional professionalism lapses; thus professionalism must result from a temporary mismatch between the individual's knowledge, judgment, or skill and the complexity of the situation in which he finds himself. Finally, the systems in which we care for patients and educate learners may either help us sustain our professional values or set us up for failure.

If we consider professionalism lapses to be either analogous to or a form of medical error, we can apply the tools that have been useful in managing medical error to the problem of professionalism lapses. Establishing a "just environment," in which people are encouraged to report professionalism challenges, lapses, and near misses can help us understand the spectrum of professionalism problems. Root-cause analysis may enable us to fully characterize the many causes of professionalism lapses. In combination, these tools can guide us in devising strategies to help all professionals and learners prevent or address professionalism lapses. Finally, the concept of active lapses (those caused by a physician) and latent lapses (those caused when the system fails to protect the vulnerable patient from the fallible physician) adds additional intervention points for leaders to consider.

Analyzing lapses: Conflicts abound and systems may set people up to fail

Analyzing articles written about professionalism challenges (difficult situations) and lapses (challenges that were not managed well) from the perspective of students, residents, faculty, practicing physicians, and scholars give insights into the root cause of professionalism lapses, as does our own experience in working with learners and faculty who have lapsed. Professionalism challenges tend to be crowded: they often require the clinician to simultaneously manage the needs and expectations of multiple people (the patient, peers, learners, faculty, nurses, administrators and others). In managing challenges, several conflicts are present (Table 1). Ginsberg and colleagues have described the challenge of values conflicts: when adhering to one professionalism value means subjugating another professionalism value. In addition to values conflicts, there may be patient conflicts: when attempting to be professional with one patient puts you at odds with another patient.[15,16] Finally, the most common cause of lapses appears to be Maslow conflicts, when adhering to a professionalism value requires that an individual subjugate his fundamental physiologic, safety, belonging, or esteem needs.[17] Maslow theorized that human beings, when faced with decisions on how to act, will predictably choose the decision that meets their deficit needs for food, water, sleep, safety, and belonging before acting selflessly.

Table 1. Conflicts Are a Frequent Cause of Professionalism Challenges	
Values conflict	An intern is expected to adhere to the professionalism value of excellence by leaving after she has been on a shift that exceeds work hours limits and to demonstrate altruism for her patient by staying to conduct a family meeting after that shift ends.
Patient conflict	A faculty member demonstrates compassion for a patient who has just received bad news by extending the length of that patient's appointment; the subsequent patient views him as unprofessional for keeping him waiting.
	A physician wants to maintain confidentiality about his patient's communicable disease, but doing so puts other of his patients at risk.
	A resident is trying to actively manage a dying cancer patient's pain and therefore must defer seeing another patient whose nonmalignant chronic pain syndrome is not well managed.
Maslow conflict	A medical student is assigned to care for an angry patient in the middle of the night; he hasn't eaten for fifteen hours and is very anxious about performing well.
Systems conflict	A resident is instructed to see all patients who are to be discharged now so that they can be out of the hospital by 11 AM. She is repeatedly called to come to the emergency room to evaluate a new admission because the emergency room resident has been told to clear out the ED before 9 AM.

The concept of latent errors, or decisions made about how health care systems are run, also has relevance to the topic of professionalism lapses. Staffing and workload issues may cause significant stress and distraction for professionals, leading to many conflicts as they attempt to serve multiple patients simultaneously. Inconsistent, ambiguous, or conflicting expectations from employers or accreditors can also cause lapses, as is the case when residents are told to always put their patients' needs above their own, but are then instructed that they must drop everything and leave when they have reached the maximum number of hours on duty. Institutional policy decisions about how clinicians are rewarded may prioritize high-volume throughput of patients over high-quality patient care and teaching. Legal policies and indemnity strategies may make it difficult for physicians and others to apologize when an error has been made. Finally, national health care decisions that leave millions uninsured or that prohibit conversations like end-of-life care may also set physicians and others up to fail.

A new perspective

With this analysis in mind, we propose a new perspective: we expect that all professionals will be deeply committed to living the values of professionalism but at times will be challenged by circumstances that are stressful and trying. To ensure that our profession meets our obligations to society, we must teach all professionals to anticipate and skillfully manage even the most challenging of professionalism circumstances. If successful, we will cultivate a generation of fully formed professionals who, as articulated by Leach, recognize that "Professionalism means going beyond the amateur in participating in the relationships . . . The fully formed professional is habitually faithful to professional values in highly complex situations."[18]

Managing a professionalism challenge requires judgment and skill

Any time you routinely expect human beings to behave in a way that is counter to human instinct or human incentive, you are dealing with a challenge of acquired competency. Thus, preparing people to be habitually faithful to professional values in these complex situations means that we must view professionalism not as a character trait but as a complex, multidimensional competency. Like other complex competencies, the competency of professionalism must follow a developmental curve[19] in which intent to comply and live values of professionalism is the entry into the profession, but mastering the skills and judgment to live professionalism despite hostile environments requires practice, reflection, and coaching. Lapses are likely to occur when the complexity of the situation exceeds the developmental level of the professional in question. Thus, an entering student can and should be able to articulate the values of professionalism in a context-free environment, but may stumble in solving a challenge that requires her to prioritize one value over another or one patient over another. A resident judged to be competent in professionalism may be able to successfully navigate a professionalism challenge between patients, but may be less adept when he is asked to do so after a long stretch of night float shifts. At the other end of the developmental spectrum, an established physician must be able to successfully navigate

16

stressful situations as well as conflicts between patients and values despite having unmet deficit needs.

Teaching the seven skills of professionalism resiliency

Dealing with professionalism as a pedagogical challenge provides new opportunities. First, we can expand our teaching about professionalism beyond descriptions of behavior we expect and into skills that foster resiliency. None of these skills are routinely taught or assessed in our conventional courses on doctor-patient relationships but should be added to all medical curricula. They focus on skills to manage self as well as skills to interact effectively with all in the health care environment. Table 2 summarizes the seven skill sets needed for professionalism resiliency.

Table 2. Seven Skills for Professional Resilience		
1.	Situational analysis	Recognize when the situation involves conflicts among values or patients and what those conflicts entail.
2.	Self awareness and self control	Recognize personal triggers and signs of personal stress/anxiety; learn to assess for these before high-stakes or stressful encounters; develop strategies to optimize personal well-being in the moment and over the long term.
3.	Alternate strategy development	Devise strategies to obtain assistance quickly.
4.	Advanced communication: diplomacy, de-escalation, conflict management	Learn techniques to interact with patients and others within the health care environment.
5.	Managing professional boundaries	Recognize the risks of boundary violations and develop skills to avoid or recover from boundary crossings.
6.	Peer coaching and intervention	Develop skills to recognize when colleagues appear to be at risk of a professionalism lapse and to intervene before the lapse occurs; learn how to counsel someone after the lapse has occurred.
7.	Effective apologies	Learn to apply the elements of a successful apology when a lapse has injured a relationship.

The first of these skills is situational analysis: helping learners and physicians to recognize when the situation in front of them is complex and may include values or patient conflicts. They must recognize the need to slow down and make an explicit decision about what to do, rather than simply responding with human instinct. There is a growing literature on the importance of switching between generally appropriate fast thinking and more methodical slow thinking that provides relevant models for this type of work.[20–22]

The second set of skills that must be inculcated comes from the emotional intelligence literature: the skills of self awareness and self control. Teaching residents and learners that they should pause and take stock of their own emotions before they deal with a predictably challenging situation can be life changing.

The third set of skills includes the ability to generate alternate strategies for action that go beyond the first instinctive response. Formal training in diplomacy, conflict de-escalation, crisis communication, and negotiation can be useful in helping professionals defuse tense situations, whether they occur between professionals or with patients. These are different skills than the usual relationship building or transactional information gathering skills that are included in doctor-patient relationship courses.

Education about and skill in identifying and maintaining appropriate professional boundaries is currently a focus in the training of psychiatry residents, but all professionals should be skilled in this competency.

A core responsibility and value of professionalism is professional self regulation: the responsibility of the profession to police itself. Physicians must be taught how to intervene when a lapse seems imminent and how to coach peers who have committed a lapse.

Finally, recognizing that lapses will occur even in the best of circumstances, we must teach our professionals how to express a genuine and effective apology if their behavior or words have injured another.

Shaping the system to support professionalism

As leaders in the health care environment, we must shape our care delivery systems to support a culture of professionalism. All, not merely those who work in education, must recognize the existence and the danger of the "hidden curriculum." We must work to develop a culture in which all welcome an intervention by a colleague if a professionalism lapse is imminent or has occurred. We should champion positive examples of professionalism so that the stories that circulate among our learners and our peers are those describing us when we are at our best, not gossiping about us when we are at our worst.[23] We must facilitate interprofessional teamwork, incorporating shared values of professionalism and welcoming support and coaching from all in the health professions. We should take steps to remove unnecessary stressors by ensuring that institutional policies and procedures reinforce rather than undermine desirable behavior.

We must devise service recovery systems for all who have been harmed by a professionalism lapse.[24] All organizations should support reflection and renewal through both environmental and event planning. Quiet rooms for professionals to go to gather their thoughts, calm down, and recommit to professionalism values should be available on all patient care units. Events that celebrate and create community are essential to establishing the positive culture of professionalism.

Recalibrating our approach to professionalism lapses in learners

As educators, we need to engage in continuous formative evaluation of professionalism. We should test professionalism skills in our learners in varied situations, both real and simulated. We should use root-cause analysis to identify and debrief professionalism lapses and to teach our learners to do the same. We need to use a developmental lens when assessing professionalism lapses in trainees so that the intervention is proportionate to the severity, and tailored to address the root cause of the lapse in the learner. Disciplinary action should be reserved for individuals who refuse to engage in honest self-reflection, are unwilling to accept responsibility for their behavior and other's perceptions of their behaviors, are resistant to coaching and counseling, or who demonstrate recidivist behavior despite educational interventions.

Encouraging continuing professionalism education

Finally, as in ethics, advances in biomedical science, care delivery, and health care economics will bring new challenges to professionalism.

Table 3. Biomedical and Social Advances that May Present Professionalism Challenges	
Risk sharing in the Affordable Care Act	May create an appearance of conflict of interest if physicians are incentivized to limit care because of costs to the system.
Returning pleiotropic results from genetic testing to patients	Physicians who disclose all possible implications of genetic testing may cause harm to patients; those who select which information to share may be charged with paternalism or lying.
Cord blood testing for perinatal diagnosis of genetic risk for adult disease	Physicians disclosing risk to parents about conditions that will not appear before adulthood may be violating patient confidentiality.

Table 3 summarizes recent advances that may have implications for appropriate professional behavior. While we have accepted the need to continuously update our biomedical knowledge, we have treated professionalism as a label that is earned once and assumed to be stable throughout the course of a career. It is time for professionalism as a renewable competency to also be reflected in continuing medical education courses.

In summary

If we wish to fulfill our commitment to society to educate and sustain health care professionals who are committed to and capable of living the values of professionalism, we can no longer afford to assume that professionalism is a character trait that is established at the time of entry into medical school. Instead, we must embrace the concept of professionalism as a complex competency. We must seek ways to prepare our physicians to exercise, adapt, and improve the judgment and skills needed to remain professional despite the dynamic and stressful environment in which health care is delivered. As a community, we must also take responsibility for shaping the systems in which we practice so that they support our core values. The work is hard, but the reward will be great if we as a profession embrace this challenge.

References

1. Smith LG. Medical professionalism and the generation gap. Am J Med 2005; 118: 439–42.

2. Heifetz R, Linsky M. Leadership on the Line: Staying Alive through the Dangers of Leading. Boston (MA): Harvard Business Review; 2002.

3. Lucey C, Souba WC. Perspective: The problem with the problem of professionalism. Acad Med 2010; 85: 1018–24.

4. Papadakis MA, Hodgson CS, Teherani A, Kohatsu ND. Unprofessional behavior in medical school is associated with subsequent disciplinary action by a state medical board. Acad Med 2004; 79: 244–49.

5. Stern DT, Frohna AZ, Gruppen LD. The prediction of professional behaviour. Med Educ 2005; 39: 75–82.

6. Albanese MA, Snow MH, Skochelak SE, et al. Assessing personal qualities in medical school admissions. Acad Med 2003; 78: 313–21.

7. Campbell EG, Regan S, Gruen RL, et al. Professionalism in medicine: Results of a national survey of physicians. Ann Intern Med 2007; 147: 795–802.

8. Huddle TS, Accreditation Council for Graduate Medical Education (ACGME). Viewpoint: Teaching professionalism: Is medical morality a competency? Acad Med. 2005; 80: 885–91.

9. Ginsburg S, Regehr G, Hatala R, et al. Context, conflict, and resolution: A newconceptual framework for evaluating professionalism. Acad Med 2000; 75

(10 Suppl): S6 –S11.

10. Ginsburg S, Regehr G, Lingard L. Basing the evaluation of professionalism on observable behaviors: A cautionary tale. Acad Med 2004; 79 (10 Suppl): S1–4.

11. Hafferty FW, Franks R. The hidden curriculum, ethics teaching, and the structure of medical education. Acad Med 1994; 69: 861–71.

12. Testerman JK. The natural history of cynicism in physicians. Acad Med 1996; 71 (10 Suppl): S43–45.

13. Burack JH, Irby DM, Carline JD, Root RK, Larson EB. Teaching compassion and respect. Attending physicians' responses to problematic behaviors. J Gen Intern Med 1999; 14: 49–55.

14. Mizrahi T. Managing medical mistakes: Ideology, insularity and accountability among internists-in-training. Soc Sci Med 1984; 19: 135–46.

15. Ginsburg S, Regehr G, Stern D, Lingard L. The anatomy of the professional lapse: Bridging the gap between traditional frameworks and students' perceptions. Acad Med 2002; 77: 516–22.

16. Ginsburg S, Regehr G, Lingard L. The disavowed curriculum: Understanding student's reasoning in professionally challenging situations. J Gen Intern Med 2003; 18: 1015–22.

17. Bryan CS. Medical professionalism and Maslow's needs hierarchy. Pharos Alpha Omega Alpha Honor Medical Soc 2005 Spring; 68: 4–10.

18. Leach DC. Professionalism: The formation of physicians. Am J Bioeth 2004 Spring; 4: 11–12.

19. Dreyfus SE, Dreyfus HL. A Five-Stage Model of the Mental Activities Involved in Directed Skill Acquisition. Available at: http://stinet.dtic.mil/cgi-bin/GetTRDoc?AD=ADA084551&Location=U2&doc=GetTRDoc.pdf.

20. Kahneman D. Thinking, Fast and Slow. New York: Farrar, Straus and Giroux; 2011.

21. Moulton CA, Regehr G, Lingard L, et al. "Slowing down when you should": Initiators and influences of the transition from the routine to the effortful. J Gastrointest Surg 2010; 14: 1019–26.

22. van Ryn M, Saha S. Exploring unconscious bias in disparities research and medical education. JAMA 2011; 306: 995–96.

23. Brater DC. Viewpoint: Infusing professionalism into a school of medicine: Perspectives from the dean. Acad Med 2007; 82: 1094–97.

24. Hickson GB, Pichert JW, Webb LE, Gabbe SG. A complementary approach to promoting professionalism: Identifying,measuring, and addressing unprofessional behaviors. Acad Med 2007; 82: 1040–48.

Chapter 3

Current Practices in Remediating Medical Students with Professionalism Lapses

Deborah Ziring, MD, Suely Grosseman, MD, PhD, and
Dennis Novack, MD

Although professionalism has been a concern for the past three decades, little is known about best practices in remediation of professionalism lapses. In 2002, in response to concerns about changes in health care delivery that were threatening physician professionalism, a collaborative effort by leaders of the American Board of Internal Medicine (ABIM) Foundation, the American College of Physicians-American Society of Internal Medicine (ACP-ASIM) Foundation, and the European Federation of Internal Medicine produced the Physician Charter.[1] This work emphasized three fundamental principles of professionalism: the primacy of patient welfare, patient autonomy, and social justice. The imperative, however, for identifying students with lapses early in their education was not fully appreciated until 2004, when Papadakis et al. linked professionalism lapses in medical students with future disciplinary action by state medical boards.[2] Subsequently, in 2008 the Liaison Committee on Medical Education (LCME) implemented Element 3.5 (previously Standard MS-31A), which requires medical schools to detail the methods used to assess and remediate professionalism in their students.[3] Yet no consensus currently exists for defining professionalism in medical education, as evidenced by Birden's 2014 systematic review of the literature on this topic (though various definitions share many essential elements).[4] In addition, assessment is complex and must take into account the individual, the existing interpersonal relationships, and the societal-environmental factors present at any given moment.[5] An individual's professionalism is dynamic, responding to competing demands and the organizational environment.[6] The importance of institutional culture toward professionalism and how lapses are handled has been previously documented by Hickson[7] and Shapiro.[8]

This chapter includes content that was first published online at
www.academicmedicine.org and will appear in the July 2015 print issue of
Academic Medicine: Ziring D, Danoff D, Grosseman S, et al. How Do Medical
Schools Identify and Remediate Professionalism Lapses in Medical Students?
A Study of U.S. and Canadian Medical Schools. *Academic Medicine*. 2015;
90 (7). doi: 10.1097/ACM.0000000000000737. Used with permission of the
Association of American Medical Colleges.

There is a growing consensus that professional formation is a developmental process.[9,10] Helping learners to recognize professionalism conflicts and to navigate resolution when such situations arise is part of this development.[11] Inevitably, some students will make mistakes from which they must learn. Still, little is known about best practices in remediation at any stage across the continuum from medical school to practice.[12] In 2011, Alpha Omega Alpha (AΩA) sponsored a think tank of experts in medical professionalism that focused on interventions and remediation strategies for medical professionalism lapses. This group called attention to the paucity of information on evidence for best practices in remediating professionalism lapses and recommended as one next step gathering data on existing practices until evidence-based research could be conducted.[13]

For many years, the educational leadership at our institution, the Drexel University College of Medicine (DUCOM) has been taking an ad hoc approach to the issues of how best to remediate and monitor our students with professionalism lapses. In 2004, Dr. Papadakis visited DUCOM and shared her work in this area. We had already been performing peer assessments with student feedback in the first year but had not established a formal process for remediating lapses throughout all four years. We also had no systematic curriculum in professionalism education. By 2010, we had a four-year longitudinal professional formation curriculum with professionalism graduation competencies. In 2012, our Professionalism Remediation Advisory Board was created to formalize the professionalism remediation process of our students. But we also wanted to know what other schools were doing: What strategies and processes have been employed among North American schools to identify and remediate lapses among medical students? Since little data existed in the literature, we undertook a study of LCME-accredited schools in the United States and Canada to analyze the current practices on professionalism lapses and remediation that will be described in this chapter.

Method

Since we were unable to identify a suitable survey instrument to collect all of the data we wanted to address in our survey, we developed one based initially on questions from Swick et al.[14] and Bennett et al.,[15] with additional questions added through an iterative process. Pilot testing was carried out at two institutions; the questionnaire was then modified to the version used for this survey. The version includes sixteen open and closed-ended questions. Questions addressed the following four areas:

1. Professionalism policies
2. Identification of students with lapses
3. Administrative response to lapses

4. Remediation practices

After the first forty-seven schools were interviewed, three additional questions regarding examples of lapses were added to identify student behaviors that triggered remediation. These three additional questions were e-mailed to all previously interviewed respondents and included during all subsequent phone interviews. The final survey questionnaire is in the Appendix.

Before recruitment of participants began, a letter of determination was sent to Drexel's IRB that determined that this project was not human subject research. Subject schools were identified using the Association of American Medical Colleges (AAMC) list of accredited schools accessed on April 25, 2012. E-mails were sent to the education deans at each school explaining the study and asking for the contact information for the key person(s) at their institution responsible for medical student professionalism remediation. Follow-up by e-mail and phone was conducted at one and two weeks after the initial e-mail. Once identified, this key person was contacted with an e-mail detailing the study and requesting participation in a thirty-minute phone interview. Once an interview was scheduled, respondents were e-mailed the questionnaire at least twenty-four hours prior to the structured phone interview. All interviews were conducted by one of two interviewers who had received three hours of training. All phone interviews were recorded and transcribed. A ten percent sample was reviewed for accuracy. Data collection occurred from June 2012 to April 2013.

A mixed-methods approach was utilized for data analysis. Quantitative data were de-identified and inserted into SPSS (IBM SPSS Statistics. Version 20. Chicago: IBM; 2012.). An impartial third party reviewed quantitative data entries. Basic descriptive analysis of this data was performed and x2 tests on select data were performed. Qualitative analysis was performed after loading transcripts into Atlas.ti (Version 7. Berlin: Scientific Software Development GmbH; 2012.), guided by procedures based on grounded theory.[16] Researchers discussed emerging results throughout the coding and analysis process to minimize the effect of a single analyst bias. Qualitative analysis was directed to three areas:

1. Anonymous reporting

2. Sharing information about struggling students (feed-forward practices)

3. Respondents' perceptions of system strengths and weaknesses

Results

Ninety-three of 153 invited schools participated (60.8%). Ninety of those schools completed the questionnaire by telephone interview, while three schools completed it in writing. Sixty-six schools (71% of sample) responded to the three additional questions regarding specific examples of professionalism lapses. Eighty-one of the ninety-three schools were located in the United States (87.1% of sample and 59.6% of eligible U.S. schools) and twelve were in Canada (12.9% of sample and 70.6% of eligible Canadian schools). Using the regional designations of the AAMC Group on Educational Affairs (GEA), response rates by region were Northeast 56.0% (28 of 50 schools), South 54% (27 of 50 schools), Central 68.6% (24 of 35 schools) and West 77.8% (14 of 18 schools). Entering class size among respondents for academic year 2012–2013 ranged from forty-two to 362 students with most schools having between 100 and 200 students.[17] Seven of the schools received their first matriculating class less than five years ago. These are identified as "new schools" in this report.

Schools' written policies and procedures regarding professionalism lapses

Most respondents (79.6%) reported that their schools had written policies and procedures regarding medical student professionalism lapses. Many of them provided those documents or links to access them. Although formal qualitative analysis of these policies is not yet available, elements commonly seen were descriptions of expectations, mechanisms for reporting lapses, and potential consequences for lapses, as well as linkage to university or other umbrella policies. While some policies contained broad generalizations about conducting oneself in a professional manner, others contained very detailed descriptions of behaviors expected, as well as specific procedures and consequences for different types of lapses.

Administrative oversight

The administrative oversight of this process was complex. We asked: When unprofessional behavior is identified and requires a response beyond immediate feedback, who is initially notified? At the majority of schools, such a lapse was reported to the course director and/or student affairs dean, often simultaneously. In about 20% of respondent schools, initial reporting was to the medical education dean. At about 5% of schools, it was initially reported to the professionalism director, promotions committee, or honor court. The course director and student affairs dean determined the course of action, devised the remediation and oversaw the remediation at the majority of schools as detailed in Table 1 below. Promotions committees had a larger role in the latter stages of this process, such as determining the action after a lapse, devising remediation, and assessing the outcome of remediation, than they did at the initial notification or oversight of remediation phases.

Person/ Committee	Notified initially about lapse	Determines action after lapse	Devises remediation	Oversees remediation	Assesses outcome of remediation
			n^a (%)^b		
Student affairs dean	69 (74.2)	54 (58.1)	46 (49.5)	48 (51.6)	45 (48.9)
Course or clerkship director	63 (67.7)	30 (32.3)	44 (47.3)	37 (39.8)	38 (41.3)
Medical education dean	19 (20.4)	26 (28.0)	17 (18.3)	19 (20.4)	16 (17.4)
Professionalism director	5 (5.4)	8 (8.6)	9 (9.7)	10 (10.8)	9 (9.8)
Promotions committee	5 (5.4)	35 (37.6)	41 (44.1)	20 (21.5)	40 (43.5)
Honor court	4 (4.3)	9 (9.7)	9 (9.7)	6 (6.5)	6 (6.5)
Medical school dean	2 (2.2)	3 (3.2)	3 (3.2)	0 (0)	3 (3.2)
Other	6 (6.5)	9 (9.7)	12 (12.9)	9 (9.7)	11 (12.0)

Table 1. Administrative Oversight of Professionalism Lapses of Medical Students among 93 U.S. and Canadian LCME-Accredited Schools (June 2012–April 2013)

[a] The count of schools in each column totals to more than 93 because some schools involved more than one administrator at a time and/or have different system pathways depending on student progress through the program (preclinical or clinical), lapse severity, and/or frequency of lapses.

[b] The denominator for percent determination is 93, not the total n in each column.

Identification of lapses

Mechanisms used to identify professionalism lapses were incident-based reporting, items on routine student evaluations, a separate professionalism course with grade, formal peer assessment, and anonymous reporting.

Eighty-eight percent of schools (82/93) used an incident-based reporting system in the preclinical years, while 92.1% (82/89) used it in the clinical years. Some respondents from new schools that did not yet have students in the clinical years could not respond to certain questions. Many schools also routinely collected information about professionalism on student evaluations. During the clinical years, 97.8% of schools (88/90) used routine student evaluations in all clerkships and courses to collect information about student professionalism. The two schools that did not collect this information for all courses/clerkships during the clinical years excluded non-patient care courses such as an intersession. Sources of information for evaluations during the clinical years were faculty, house staff, other health care professionals, patients, and/or their families. During the preclinical years, 43.5% of schools (40/92) used routine student evaluations in all courses to collect professionalism information, and another 37.0% (34/92) collected this information in some courses.

Fifteen percent of respondents indicated that they had a separate professionalism course and grade. Forty-five percent of schools (41/92) used formal peer assessment in the preclinical years, while 16.7% (15/90) used it during the clinical years. All schools that used peer assessment during the clinical years also used it during the preclinical years. Frequency of peer assessment at schools that used it was quite variable. At some schools assessment was performed annually, while at other schools repeated assessments provided multiple data points throughout the year, often at the end of a module or block.

Half of the respondent schools (46/92) reported that they had a mechanism for anonymous reporting (i.e., no information about reporter required). The existence of an anonymous reporting system was not statistically different among schools in different geographic regions ($x2=3.67$, $p=0.30$) or class size ($x2=3.25$, $p=0.52$). However, qualitative analysis indicated that assessing anonymous reporting was not straightforward. For example, some schools with an anonymous reporting system indicated that no action could be taken on a report submitted anonymously; therefore no help could be directed toward a student with a professionalism lapse unless the lapsing student had a chance to address the reporting student's concerns. Such a system effectively negates any practical utility of an anonymous reporting system. In addition, many schools with a so-called anonymous reporting system were actually using a confidential system in which a reporting student was identified to the administration handling the report but remained unknown to the student reported.

Most common lapses cited

Sixty-six respondents of the ninety-three schools (71%) reported their perceptions about the three most common professionalism lapses at their institutions, resulting in 183 responses. We categorized these responses using Papadakis' proposed categorization of lapses, which is based on four behavioral domains (presented at the 2013 AΩA Professionalism Meeting).[18] These categories are described more completely in Chapter 1 of this monograph, but are:

1. Responsibility (e.g., late or absent for assigned activities, missing deadlines, unreliable)

2. Diminished capacity for self-improvement (e.g., arrogant, hostile, or defensive behavior)

3. Relationship with patients, including communication with patients

4. Relationship with health care environment (e.g., testing irregularities, falsifying data, or impaired communication with team).

Lapses in responsibility were most common (n=102, 55.7%), followed by lapses related to the health care environment (n=59, 32.2%), diminished capacity for self-improvement (n=18, 9.8%), and lapses in relationship with patients (n=4, 2.2%). Academic dishonesty, including cheating and plagiarism, accounted for twelve (7%) of total responses, but made up 20% of the lapses in the domain of relationship with health care environment (12/59).

Certain professionalism lapses were grounds for dismissal at some schools and not remediated. These included committing a felony, falsifying patient information, falsifying information on a residency application, forging a prescription, not reporting for clinical call, or research misconduct endangering safety. Some respondents reported cheating on an exam as grounds for dismissal, while others remediated this behavior. In addition, respondents cited an ongoing pattern of repeated offenses or lack of adherence to a prescribed remediation plan as potential grounds for dismissal.

Remediation strategies

Schools remediating professionalism lapses used a variety of strategies, as listed below in Table 2. Schools were asked to include all strategies that they have employed for remediation regardless of the frequency with which they used that strategy.

Table 2. Strategies for Remediation among 93 U.S. and Canadian LCME-Accredited Schools (June 2012–April 2013)	
Strategy	n (%)[a]
Mandated mental health evaluation/treatment	74 (82.2%)
Complete professionalism assignment	66 (73.3%)
Mandated professionalism mentor	66 (73.3%)
Counseling for stress or anger management	65 (72.2%)
Repeat part or all of course/clerkship	59 (64.8%)
Mandated community service	15 (16.6%)
Other	04 (04.4%)
[a] Percent is calculated using n=90 schools, since three schools had new programs and had not yet remediated any students.	

In general, schools combined a number of strategies to remediate professionalism lapses depending on the particular details of the lapse. A number of respondents indicated that decisions regarding remediation were determined on a case-by-case basis rather than by a formalized structured approach. Many respondents stressed the critical importance of initial dialogue with the student to evaluate student stress and mental health in addition to the details surrounding the lapse when devising a remediation plan.

In regard to mental health evaluation and treatment, some respondents referred students to school-employed practitioners, while others utilized external programs established for physicians but not specifically designed for students. Similarly, stress management and counseling was conducted through either internal school-based programs or through "arms-length" external programs.

The details of how mandated professionalism mentors were employed varied considerably. Individuals assigned as mentors included deans, faculty members, advisors, course directors, or professionalism program directors. Mentor-mentee meeting frequency was individualized depending on the situation. The number of follow-up meetings varied from a total of three meetings to as often as weekly for the duration of the student's enrollment at the medical school. The mentor and mentee most often spent their time together discussing the specific professionalism lapse, reviewing completed professionalism assignments, and/or discussing general professionalism issues.

The assignments employed for remediation fell largely into two categories: reading and writing broadly about general professionalism issues or focusing selectively on the specific behavioral lapse. Some examples were directed reading with reflective writing, doing a literature review culminating in a paper/presentation, or reviewing targeted videos of professionalism lapses and critiquing them. In addition, some schools required students to review their school's policies relevant to the lapse or assist with developing new policies if no explicit policy existed. This strategy was mentioned several times—for instance, in developing or expanding social media policies. Other assignments included a required public apology to the group affected by the lapse or a private apology to an individual. Attendance at disciplinary committee meetings was sometimes required, which could be at the school, hospital, or state level. One school required a student with academic dishonesty to write a reflective piece from a future patient's point of view on finding out about the student's lapse during medical school.

When professionalism behavioral objectives were not met, instead of requiring the student to repeat part or all of a course/clerkship, some schools assigned an additional course or clerkship including, for example, a special bio-psychosocial elective with a focus on professionalism.

The respondents that employed community service as remediation reported that they used it in two general circumstances: when the intent was to make the student better understand the physician's roles and responsibilities within the community by assigning him to work with a disadvantaged group, or for someone considered to be lacking in empathy. One problem in applying this strategy is that organizations often do not want someone mandated to serve instead of a willing volunteer.

In addition to these specific strategies, other elements included the following. Some respondents issued a behavioral or remediation contract to students for lapses requiring remediation. Typically these documents outlined clear behavioral expectations that the student was required to meet, as well as the consequences for violation, including the potential for dismissal. Some schools officially put students on probation when they were undergoing professionalism remediation. Some respondents stated that if they put a student on probation, it was automatically noted on their Dean's letter for residency, but others expressed reluctance to include this information. The effect of academic suspension or repeating coursework that could result in delayed graduation and impact the residency application cycle was also mentioned as a consideration in the remediation process.

Although respondents largely employed the same range of strategies for professionalism remediation, the responses at different schools for similar lapses were quite variable. For example, for a lapse regarding cheating, some schools allowed the student to retake of the exam under supervision without further consequences, other schools required professionalism remediation, while still others dismissed the student outright.

Adding to this variability in handling lapses was the school's culture toward professionalism lapses. Some schools had a more punitive culture that relied on strong warnings and consequences for violations, including dismissal rather than remediation. Other schools took a developmental view and conveyed the attitude that lapses were a natural part of professional formation and an opportunity for education. In addition, some schools expressed more tolerance in the preclinical years regarding tardiness and other lapses of responsibility than during the clinical years when patient care was involved. Consider the following two representative quotes of these different views:

"Stern warnings are the most effective form of remediation."

"Most critical is to understand that these are young people who need professional development and not punishment. They are not professionals yet, they are training to be professionals."

Feed-forward practices

Forty-nine schools (52.7%) reported that they did forward feed information about professionalism lapses, while thirty-nine (41.9%) did not. Five schools (5.4%) indicated that decisions regarding forward notification depended on the stage of training and type of lapse. For example, they did not forward feed information on lapses of responsibility such as tardiness or dress code infractions, particularly during the preclinical years, but did share this information if patient safety was involved.

Feeding forward of information about students who had lapsed usually occurred via course/clerkship directors and did not go to the faculty member directly supervising the student. Feed-forward practices showed no statistically significant differences between schools in different geographic regions ($x2=5.83$, $p=0.44$) and among different class sizes ($x2=7.19$, $p=0.52$).

Qualitative analysis of responses related to forward feeding policies revealed more complexities in the decision to forward feed, practices used to forward feed, and some of the considerations in employing or not employing a forward feeding policy. First, it was clear that more schools forward feed information about lapses than the quantitative data suggest. This may be related to how respondents understood the question. Respondents who reported that their schools did not generally forward feed information stipulated instances in which they would (e.g., if patient safety was a concern). In those instances they typically did so only to individuals who did not directly supervise a student to avoid any grading bias. For example, one respondent who reported they did not forward feed qualified it by saying,

"There's no blanket rule. It depends on the nature of the incident and the level of confidentiality, which wins out in that particular situation."

One of the most common themes related to forward feeding was doing so in order to help students rather than punish them.

"[Previously problematic] behavior is tracked between clerkships. That information is passed onto the next clerkship. 'John Doe struggled with such and such, place him with a strong mentor.' In a supportive, not [punitive] way. It's more of, how can we put him with a good role model who will give him feedback early and continue the [supportive] environment?"

Often forward feeding did not follow a written protocol but was conducted through discussion in monthly course/clerkship director meetings. This tied into the idea of helping students and making sure they were supported as they moved forward; some schools did not consider this a formal feed-forward policy, however.

"We do have a meeting every month with the Clerkship Chairs and Course Chairs from the pre-clinical years. We do share the physicianship information and often will pick . . . the site where that student is going to be for a clerkship based on the level of supervision we know is present at that site."

Creating biases because of forward feeding was a common concern. For some schools this led to a policy against forward feeding.

"This is a delicate problem if somebody has professionalism difficulties. We think it's probably not a good idea [to feed forward]. Somebody having academic difficulties, that information gets passed forward. But somebody having professionalism problems, we try to have a clean slate going on to another clerkship, as an example."

Overall, almost all schools did discuss some instances in which they would forward feed information about professionalism lapses, even if their general policies were not to do so.

Faculty issues

At almost all respondent schools, faculty members were expected to directly address professionalism lapses with students when they occurred. This was a written policy at twenty-seven schools (29%) and an expectation at sixty schools (64.5%). Thirty-two schools (42.4%) had a formal faculty development program to train faculty for this role. We included all schools that performed any faculty development in this tally, including schools that did not have robust programs as well as those that had optional programs such as annual faculty development seminars on this topic.

Criteria for success

Whatever the remediation strategy, the criteria for successful remediation were not well defined. Success could be determined by the course/clerkship director who directly supervised the student, an assigned professionalism mentor, or by a promotions committee that officially voted on this issue. Respondents that used a behavioral contract cited the benefit of using that contract to outline what constituted success at the beginning of the remediation process to minimize the issue of variable perspectives of success.

Participants' perceived strengths of their remediation systems

Most strengths identified could be placed into the following four main themes:

1. Catching minor offenses early to help students before problems escalate
2. Emphasizing professionalism school-wide
3. System focusing on helping students rather than punishing them
4. Assuring transparency and good communication

Many respondents that focused on catching minor offenses early had employed a variant of the University of California, San Francisco, Physicianship Evaluation system. Some respondents emphasized professionalism through formalized teaching strategies, weaving components of professionalism education and standards throughout the curriculum, or simply working on the culture surrounding identification and reporting of lapses so that it was seen as less negative. One respondent noted their progress in emphasizing professionalism,

> "I think people are much more aware of professionalism. They're more aware that they can comment on it and address it. The students are more aware that we care about it and they're actually doing a bit more kind of peer assessment and reporting on each other when the lapses are significant. I think the structure is forming where people know how to bump up concerns around professionalism and activate our Academic Progress Committee more frequently."

Emphasizing professionalism and re-orienting school culture to one that supports rather than punishes students who lapse was also commonly noted among system strengths. As one respondent nicely summarized why professionalism systems should focus on helping students and catching offenses early,

"Sometimes students don't understand how to act in the culture of a hospital as well as are stressed out, tired and worried about grades and they sometimes do things in the heat of the moment that they normally wouldn't do."

Many respondents noted that transparent policies including clear professionalism expectations of students and consequences of lapses were critical to ensuring students understood the importance of professionalism both during school and for their future careers.

Participants' perceived weaknesses of their remediation systems

Four major themes were identified as system weaknesses. These were:
1. Reluctance to report (among both students and faculty)
2. Lack of faculty training
3. Unclear policies
4. Remediation ineffective

Factors cited for reluctance to report were faculty discomfort in determining the seriousness of the problem, the increased workload that reporting creates for them, concern about harming the student's future, that a witnessed lapse seems minor, and fear of repercussions.

Reluctance to report can work directly against early identification of a problem that could be easily addressed and remediated. One respondent noted that their school's major weakness was

". . . reluctance of [faculty] to step forward and meet with students directly about professionalism incidents. I think . . . , things get escalated too far that maybe an earlier intervention could have had a more positive outcome."

Many respondents felt that reluctance to report, at least among faculty, could be overcome with better faculty training, which was identified as a system weakness. The challenge of training clinical faculty with typically high turnover rates was cited by several schools as problematic. Some respondents felt faculty reluctance to report could also be overcome with clearer policies so that both students and faculty better understood expectations. A few respondents noted that the problem of defining professionalism itself leads to policy murkiness.

"There are some physicians in practice who work with our institution who are not fond of the term professionalism. They feel that it's being used too loosely and doesn't give the students an adequate and clear definition of what the expectations are and how those are measured and what that means."

Respondents commonly reported that their administrations struggled with remediation in a larger sense. Some of them felt that remediation simply did not work for specific lapses or certain students. One respondent noted debate at the institution over how to remediate issues resulting from certain personality types.

"I think those students . . . who are arrogant, really arrogant, or who are narcissistic . . . There are certain personality types that can figure out how to make it through what we do for remediation but who, I think, will never be beacons for professionalism. And I worry about that. We last month voted on dismissing a student on professionalism, you know? A student, who just has been followed by the Promotions Committee for two years. And was in a contract and still is exhibiting this very arrogant [behavior]. So, unfortunately, I'm not sure if we've found a way to really remediate those students who I'm most concerned about."

Beyond expectations and policies

One respondent noted that understanding professionalism and making systems work can be about more than expectations and policies. It is important to remember the "cultural" differences between students and faculty and how those will be constantly evolving as programs grow and change through time.

"What students understand to be professionalism and what faculty consider to be professionalism can be of some variance that needs to be considered (cultural differences). Faculty can make assumptions of what the incoming students should know already in terms of professionalism and that might not be the case because everyone is coming from different generational perspectives, so, they have to take advantage of the opportunities to turn incidents into learning events to teach students what faculty expect in certain circumstances."

Conclusions and discussion

The current study is the first to take a comprehensive look at medical schools' remediation practices. The quality and extent of a school's remediation system is crucial because it signals to both students and faculty the school's commitment to the professional development of its students. Student affairs deans and course directors are responsible for addressing the great majority of lapses. It is notable that a minority of schools had a director overseeing professionalism education and remediation. The findings revealed considerable variation in the policies and procedures to identify and intervene in addressing lapses in professionalism. The identification of lapses varied among schools, with some having few, and others very elaborate mechanisms for identifying these students. All of these mechanisms are limited, though, as our respondents suggested, by differing conceptions of professionalism among faculty and students, reluctance to report, and mistrust of the reporting system. Though peer assessment has been found to be a valuable means of providing feedback to students and faculty,[19] fewer than half of responding schools used this method in the preclinical years, and only a small percentage during the clinical years.

Using the organizational framework for lapses based on the behavioral domains proposed by Papadakis at the 2013 AΩA professionalism meeting,[18] lapses in responsibility were reported by our respondents as most common. In her 2005 work, Papadakis et al. found that lapses in the domain of responsibility had the highest odds ratio of 8.5 for subsequent disciplinary action.[20] Although individually seen as "minor" lapses, identification of these lapses with formative feedback to students when they occur would be important to promote correction of problematic behaviors and connect the implications of behavior with the expected professionalism ideals in the practice of medicine. In addition, Ainsworth found that student response when confronted with the report of a professionalism lapse was a better predictor of subsequent lapses than was the type of behavior that triggered the report. Students with diminished capacity to recognize that their behaviors were unprofessional or who were unwilling to accept responsibility for their behaviors were at high risk for subsequent lapses.[21] Tracking these "minor" lapses longitudinally so that patterns could be discerned, with remediation and monitoring when repetitive, would likely be beneficial.

Some of the remediation practices employed were designed to emphasize this connection to professionalism ideals, such as those employing reflective writing assignments and meetings with professionalism mentors. Also, it is clear that faculty often "diagnose" the root cause of professionalism lapses to be mental health problems, as evidenced by the frequent usage of mandated mental health evaluations and counseling for stress and anger management. This is not surprising considering the high rates of depression, anxiety, and burnout among medical students.[22–24]

Several study limitations should be noted here. First, while our response rate was better than many comparable studies,[25] the study may be subject to sampling bias, including voluntary response and nonresponse biases. The former may have led to inclusion of schools more interested in professionalism, while the latter may have led to data that reflects schools most active in professionalism reporting and remediation. Second, though we attempted to minimize the effect of "undercoverage" by considering AAMC region and class size, our sample may not be truly reflective of all schools. Third, the complexity of the remediation process and wording of some questions may have led to confusion among respondents, given their variable levels of expertise.

Despite these limitations, our study has significant strengths. By compiling this data, we have created the first inventory of current practices for identifying and remediating professionalism lapses among medical students. We have called attention to the current unnecessary variability within and among schools that would be well served by consensus guidelines for best practices in this area. The Association of Faculties of Medicine in Canada (AFMC) has recently published such consensus guidelines for designing professionalism remediation for undergraduates, postgraduate trainees, and faculty members in Canada.[26]

We think that the themes we have identified as system strengths may hold promise in formulating such a best practices approach to remediation including:

1. Catching minor offenses early to help students before problems escalate requires that a graded response to lapses be utilized.

2. Emphasizing professionalism school-wide, with clear definitions of expected behaviors and consequences, including remediation when students fall short.

3. Focusing on helping students rather than punishing them, so that personal and professional growth is supported.

4. Assurance of transparency and good communication, with a well-defined process for reporting and tracking.

Tackling faculty reluctance to report through robust training so that faculty members understand the significance of "minor" lapses and feel more comfortable having those initial crucial conversations when sub-optimal professional behaviors are encountered would foster early identification of students with lapses so that they could be helped. A longitudinal view of student performance in this area would need to be included in a best-practices approach so that patterns of lapses could be identified and monitored. Since the responsibility for professionalism remediation seems diffuse at many institutions, specific responsibility for this role needs to be clearly defined, with resources to mentor and track student progress. It is clear that feed-forward policies are not straightforward and consensus on this issue is lacking, as has been previously reported in the literature.[27–30] The components of this approach are very similar to those previously outlined by Hickson on the infrastructure necessary for promoting reliability and professional accountability.[7]

We recommend several immediate next steps:

1. Create an online repository of robust examples of school policies and procedures, behavioral contracts, and remediation assignments so schools can easily share successful practices and build on existing resources.

2. Provide robust faculty training to enhance skills and knowledge in addressing lapses and early reporting.

3. Explore further the risks and benefits of feed-forward practices.

4. Investigate the factors contributing to underreporting so they can be addressed.

In the long term, we recommend effectiveness studies of identification and remediation strategies as measured through student outcomes.

Acknowledgments

The authors thank the following colleagues who contributed to the original survey project described in this chapter: Deborah Langer, MPA; Deborah Danoff, MD; Amanda Esposito, MS4; Mian Kouresch Jan, MS4; and Steven Rosenzweig, MD. We would also like to thank our colleagues at all of the participating institutions for their thoughtful contributions to this work and their insightful comments.

References

1. ABIM Foundation, American Board of Internal Medicine; ACP-ASIM Foundation, American College of Physicians-American Society of Internal Medicine; European Federation of Internal Medicine. Medical professionalism in the new millennium: a physician charter. Ann Intern Med 2002; 136: 243–46.

2. Papadakis MA, Hodgson CS, Teherani A, Kohatsu ND. Unprofessional behavior in medical school is associated with subsequent disciplinary action by a state medical board. Acad Med 2004; 79: 244–49.

3. Liaison Committee on Medical Education. Functions and Structure of a Medical School: Standards for Accreditation of Medical Education Programs Leading to the M.D. Degree. Washington DC: Liaison Committee on Medical Education; 2014. Available at: http://www.lcme.org/publications/2015-16-functions-and-structure-march-2014.doc.

4. Birden H, Glass N, Wilson I, Harrison M, et al. Defining professionalism in medical education: A systematic review. Med Teach 2014; 36: 47–61.

5. Hodges BD, Ginsburg S, Cruess R, et al. Assessment of professionalism: Recommendations from the Ottawa 2010 Conference. Med Teach 2011; 33: 354–63.

6. Lucey C, Souba WC. Perspective: The problem with the problem of professionalism. Acad Med 2010; 85: 1018–24.

7. Hickson GB, Pichert JW, Webb LE, Gabbe SG. A complementary

approach to promoting professionalism: Identifying, measuring, and addressing unprofessional behaviors. Acad Med 2007; 82: 1040–48.

8. Shapiro J, Whittemore AW, Tsen LC. Instituting a culture of professionalism: The establishment of a center for professionalism and peer support. Jt Comm J Qual Patient Saf 2014; 40: 168–77.

9. Parker M, Luke H, Zhang J, et al. The "pyramid of professionalism": Seven years of experience with an integrated program of teaching, developing, and assessing professionalism among medical students. Acad Med 2008; 83: 733–41.

10. Rabow MW, Remen RN, Parmelee DX, Inui TS. Professional formation: Extending medicine's lineage of service into the next century. Acad Med 2010; 85: 310–17.

11. Cruess RL, Cruess SR, Steinert Y, editors. Teaching Medical Professionalism. New York: Cambridge University Press; 2008.

12. Hauer KE, Ciccone A, Henzel TR, et al. Remediation of the deficiencies of physicians across the continuum from medical school to practice: A thematic review of the literature. Acad Med 2009; 84: 1822–32.

13. Papadakis MA, Paauw DS, Hafferty FW, et al. Perspective: The education community must develop best practices informed by evidence-based research to remediate lapses of professionalism. Acad Med 2012; 87: 1694–98.

14. Swick HM, Szenas P, Danoff D, Whitcomb ME. Teaching professionalism in undergraduate medical education. JAMA 1999; 282: 830–32.

15. Bennett AJ, Roman B, Arnold LM, et al. Professionalism deficits among medical students: Models of identification and intervention. Acad Psychiatry 2005; 29: 426–32.

16. Charmaz K. Grounded Theory in the 21st Century: Applications for Advancing Social Justice Studies. In: Denzin NK, Lincoln YS, editors. The Sage Handbook of Qualitative Research. 3rd Edition. Thousand Oaks (CA): Sage Publications; 2005: 507–35.

17. Barzansky B, Etzel SI. Medical schools in the United States, 2012-2013. JAMA 2013; 310: 2319–27.

18. Papadakis M. Classifying lapses of professionalism around domains; An organizational tool to determining best practices for remediation. Alpha Omega Alpha Honor Medical Society Professionalism Meeting. New York; 2013.

19. Shue CK, Arnold L, Stern DT. Maximizing participation in peer assessment of professionalism: The students speak. Acad Med 2005; 80 (10 Suppl): S1–S5.

20. Papadakis MA, Teherani A, Banach MA, et al. Disciplinary action by medical boards and prior behavior in medical school. N Engl J Med 2005; 353: 2673–82.

21. Ainsworth M, Szauter K. Classifying student responses to reports of unprofessional behavior: A method for assessing likelihood of repetitive problems. Association of American Medical Colleges Medical Education Meeting. Philadelphia; 2013. https://www.aamc.org/download/357820/data/

professionalismainsworth16.pdf.

22. Dyrbye LN, Harper W, Moutier C, et al. A multi-institutional study exploring the impact of positive mental health on medical students' professionalism in an era of high burnout. Acad Med 2012; 87: 1024–31.

23. Dyrbye LN, Massie FS Jr, Eacker A, et al. Relationship between burnout and professional conduct and attitudes among US medical students. JAMA 2010; 304: 1173–80.

24. Dyrbye LN, Thomas MR, Shanafelt TD. Systematic review of depression, anxiety, and other indicators of psychological distress among U.S. and Canadian medical students. Acad Med 2006; 81: 354–73.

25. Baruch Y. Survey response rate levels and trends in organizational research. Human Relations 2008; 61: 1139–60.

26. Association of Faculties of Medicine of Canada. Consensus Guidelines on Designing Professionalism Remediation. Ottawa; 2013. https://www.afmc.ca/pdf/committees/BOARD2013-IGProfessionalism.pdf.

27. Cleary L. "Forward feeding" about students' progress: The case for longitudinal, progressive, and shared assessment of medical students. Acad Med 2008; 83: 800.

28. Cohen GS, Blumberg P. Investigating whether teachers should be given assessments of students made by previous teachers. Acad Med 1991; 66: 288–89.

29. Cox SM. "Forward feeding" about students' progress: Information on struggling medical students should not be shared among clerkship directors or with students' current teachers. Acad Med 2008; 83: 801.

30. Frellsen SL, Baker EA, Papp KK, Durning SJ. Medical school policies regarding struggling medical students during the internal medicine clerkships: Results of a national survey. Acad Med 2008; 83: 876–81.

Appendix: Survey Instrument

Interview Unique Identifier:

Date/Time of Phone Interview:

Person(s) Conducting Interview:

Statement at beginning of interview: The goal of this project is to gather information about the current status of professionalism remediation in undergraduate medical education in the U.S. and Canada. We are inviting all AAMC member schools to participate. We would like to speak to you for no more than 30 minutes. All materials gathered will be confidential. The data collected will only be used in the aggregate with no specific schools identified. However, if a particular school has an exceptional program in this area, they may be contacted separately for permission to identify their school and program. At the end of our work, we will provide a draft of our final paper.

We would like to record this phone interview in case we need it for further review during our study. May I have your permission to record this interview?

__Yes   __No

Would you like us to read you the questions off the survey, or would you like to read it yourself and answer the question?

Part I. Your school's policies and documents

1. How may we get a link to, or copy of, your school's professionalism graduation competencies (exit objectives)?

2. Does your school have a student code of conduct that is posted on the web, included in your student handbook, or made available to students in some other way?

   __Yes   __No

3. Does your school have a written policy for responding to unprofessional behavior incidents? This may include a list of trigger or sentinel events. It may include criteria for escalation of response, remediation, censure, penalty or automatic dismissal.

   __Yes   __No

   Would it be possible to receive a copy of these documents for our research?

Part II. How your school identifies students with professionalism issues

4. Should a faculty member or administrator witness a student behaving unprofessionally, is there a policy or an expectation that the faculty member or administrator will provide direct feedback to the student?

   ___Yes, a formal policy   ___Yes, an expectation   ___No

5. What are the three most common unprofessional behaviors identified at your school?

6. If unprofessional behaviors require a response that goes beyond direct feedback given by the individual who witnessed it, how are these students identified for the next level of response? **Please check all that apply**.

a) **Preclinical years**:

    I) *Incidence Based Reporting*: Do you have incident-based reporting of unprofessional behavior?

        __Yes __No

        Who is this information reported to (what is his or her title)?

    II) *Routine Periodic Evaluation of Professionalism*: **Types of collection mechanisms**

    Do you use standard or routine course evaluations that include professionalism information?

    a. Does not use

    b. Use for ALL courses

    c. Use for SOME courses

        Is there a separate professionalism course for which students receive a separate professional evaluation?

        __Yes __No

        If yes, please explain the course and how they are evaluated:

        Do you utilize formal peer-assessments?

        __Yes __No

        If yes, please explain how these assessments occur and how often:

b) **Clinical years**:

    I) *Incidence Based Reporting*: Do you have incident-based reporting of unprofessional behavior?

        __Yes __No

        Who is this information reported to (what is his or her title)?

II) *Routine Periodic Evaluation of Professionalism*: **Types of collection mechanisms**

Do you use standard or routine course evaluations that include professionalism information?

a. Does not use

b. Use for ALL courses

c. Use for SOME courses

Is there a separate professionalism course for which students receive a separate professional evaluation?

__Yes __No

If yes, please explain the course and how they are evaluated:

Is professionalism a component of every clinical evaluation form?

__Yes __No

Do you utilize formal peer-assessments?

__Yes __No

If yes, please explain how these assessments occur and how often:

III) Do other individuals, such as house staff, patients, and/or nurses, provide feedback about professionalism of students? How?

IV) Is the process different when a student is on an away elective?

c) **Does the school have a mechanism for anonymous reporting of unprofessional student behaviors?**

__Yes __No

If yes, please describe:

Part III: Response to unprofessional behavior

7. When unprofessional behavior is identified and requires a response beyond immediate feedback, who is initially notified?

a) Course or clerkship director

b) Student Affairs dean

c) Faculty Director of Professionalism Program

d) Dean

e) Other

8. Who determines the course of action to be taken? This might include determination that the incident is resolved, referral to Honor Court, referral to Promotions Committee, recommendation for dismissal, or initiation of remediation?

   a) Course or clerkship director

   b) Student Affairs dean

   c) Faculty Director of Professionalism Program

   d) Dean

   e) Other

9. Regarding the response to unprofessional behavior, please explain the role of:

   a) Honor Court/Student Professional Conduct Committee

   b) Promotions Committee

   c) Committee of Faculty or Administrators convened specifically to review unprofessional conduct

   d) Student Affairs Dean

   e) Other Individuals or Groups (please identify by title)

10. Do you have a faculty development program to train faculty how to respond to professionalism issues?

    __Yes __No

    If yes, please describe:

Part IV: Remediation

11. When a student is referred to remediation, who devises the remediation?

    a) Course or clerkship director

    b) Student Affairs dean

    c) Faculty Director of Professionalism Program

    d) Dean

    e) Other

12. Who oversees the remediation?

    a) Course or clerkship director

    b) Student Affairs dean

    c) Faculty Director of Professionalism Program

    d) Dean

    e) Other

13. Who assesses the outcome of the remediation?

    a) Course or clerkship director

    b) Student Affairs dean

    c) Faculty Director of Professionalism Program

    d) Dean

    e) Other

    Explanation:

14. What strategies are utilized for remediation of unprofessional behaviors?

    a) Repeat course/clerkship

    b) Repeat course/clerkship with faculty supervision regarding professionalism deficit

    c) Mandated professionalism mentor:

    Who is assigned?

    How often do they meet?

    d) Stress management counseling

    e) Remediation curriculum or assignment

    f) Mandated mental health evaluation/treatment

    g) Community Service

    h) Other:

    Explanation/Please provide an example so we can better understand your process.

15. If a student has professionalism difficulties, is this information made available to future supervisors?

    __Yes __No

    If yes, explain the process of notification at your institution:

16. If a student has a significant professionalism incident, is there a standard, monitoring process moving forward?

    __Yes __No

    If yes, please describe:

17. What are some examples of the least serious unprofessional behaviors that require remediation?

18. What are some examples of the most serious unprofessional behaviors that require remediation?

19. What is working well with your current professionalism remediation strategies and what do you see not working so well?

3. Current Practices in Remediating Medical Students with Professionalism Lapses

---

This concludes our interview. Thank you very much for taking the time to share the information on professionalism remediation at your school. We greatly appreciate it.

Is there anyone else we should contact at your school?

Name_____

Title_____

Email contact_____

Phone number_____

Do you have any questions?

Models

Chapter 4

Review of Current Models for Remediation of Professionalism Lapses

Sheryl A. Pfeil, MD, and Douglas S. Paauw, MD

Professionalism is one of the most basic tenets of medical practice. It is one of the ACGME core competencies and an expectation of every medical student, resident, and practicing physician. Professionalism encompasses core professional beliefs and values, and there is an assumption that all persons entering the medical profession should have the aptitude and commitment to behave in a manner consistent with this value climate.[1] The belief that the medical profession should be held accountable to standards that are developed, declared, and enforced by the profession itself is also a promise to society.[2,3]

The authors of the 2010 Carnegie report assert that professional identity formation—the development of professional values, actions, and aspirations—should be one of the four pillars of medical education.[4] Despite widespread agreement regarding the critical importance of teaching professionalism in the medical curriculum and the importance of addressing unprofessional behaviors, there has been no clear consensus on best practices with regard to the assessment of competency and remediation of below-standard performance.[1,5–8] On an individual level, professionalism is not a dichotomous trait but rather a behavioral response that can be challenged by stressors and competing professional priorities.[9–11] Furthermore, lapses can be a part of learning, and learners require education and guidance before becoming full professionals.[1]

Call to action

The expert participants in the 2011 Alpha Omega Alpha-sponsored think tank on medical professionalism focused on interventions and remediation of professionalism lapses, with a consensus call to gather existing practices on interventions and remediation that are used for medical students, residents, faculty, and practicing physicians, and to evaluate existing remediation practices via formal research.[1] While data is still lacking on best practices for the remediation of professionalism, there is general agreement that remediation should be profession-led, that it should involve a diagnosis of the problem(s) and development of a learning plan, that instruction and remediation activities need to occur, and that some form of reassessment or follow up is needed to evaluate the adequacy of the intervention.[12–14] In this section, we outline some of the reported practices for remediation of unprofessional behaviors with examples from the published literature and from the authors' experiences.

Programs for remediation of unprofessional behavior

The Vanderbilt University School of Medicine has established an approach for identifying, measuring, and addressing unprofessional behaviors.[15] The Vanderbilt model is graduated, based on the severity of the unprofessional behavior, with physician behaviors and corresponding interventions stepped as a pyramid. The base of the pyramid includes the vast majority of physicians who consistently behave in a professional manner. Ascending up the pyramid, the next group encompasses those physicians who have a single unprofessional incident. These incidents are addressed by a conversation that serves as an informal intervention. The next step up the pyramid is when unprofessional or disruptive behaviors recur as an apparent pattern. This pattern is addressed by an awareness intervention that involves compiling and sharing data that sets the physician apart from his or her peers. Most physicians respond and make appropriate behavioral adjustments. However, a small proportion of professionals seem unable or unwilling to respond to an awareness intervention and develop a persistent pattern of unprofessional behavior. These physicians require an authority intervention, with an improvement and evaluation plan and ongoing accountability. Finally, there are the small numbers of physicians at the tip of the pyramid who, failing to respond to interventions, require disciplinary action and restriction or termination of privileges and appropriate reporting to other entities. Other key aspects of the Vanderbilt program include a supportive institutional infrastructure that involves leadership commitment to addressing unprofessional behaviors, available surveillance tools, and training and resources for addressing unprofessional behavior.

The Center for Professionalism and Peer Support at the Brigham and Women's Hospital (CPPS) is another exemplar program for addressing unprofessional behavior.[16] The CPPS does hear concerns about medical student unprofessional behavior, but most reported concerns are about physicians. The CPPS process, as previously outlined by Papadakis et al.,[1] involves five steps. The first two steps are the reporting of the concern to the CPPS and the investigation of the concern. The reporting conversation is confidential, and the reporter is allowed to choose how to move forward with the complaint, usually allowing the CPPS to further investigate the concern. Multisource interviews are conducted to determine the validity of the complaint and to obtain comprehensive input about the behavior concern. The third step is a feedback conversation with the individual of concern. The CPPS investigator and the individual's supervising physician meet with the individual to present feedback and to hear the individual's viewpoint. The focus is on the behavior, and there is a clear expectation for behavioral change. A caring but straightforward approach is used, acknowledging the frequent need for a combination of personal responsibility for behavior change and system change to facilitate a less stressful environment. The specific behaviors that need improvement are summarized, and information is provided as to how the institution will follow up to assure that the behavioral changes have occurred. Resources such as personal coaching or educational resources are offered at this juncture, but the individual decides how he or she can best facilitate the behavior change.

If subsequent lapses occur, the process moves to the fourth step. At this step, the institutional administration becomes involved, with a team that may include a member of the CPPS, the chief medical officer, the department chair, or program director. Members of the administration team meet with the individual to inform the person that the unprofessional behavior has continued and that his or her institutional appointment and employment are at risk. Interventions such as personal coaching, behavioral programs, or an external evaluation may be required. The fifth step in the process involves completing the loop by communicating with the reporter of the complaint. This communication is balanced by the competing need to maintain the privacy of the individual about whom the concerns were raised. The reporter is informed that the institution is addressing the concerns and that he or she should inform the institution should the behavior continue or should there be retaliation. This process demonstrates that professionalism concerns are taken seriously by the institution, and that the value of professional behavior and culture of professionalism are supported.[1]

Both the Vanderbilt University disruptive behavior pyramid and the Brigham and Women's Hospital program predominantly focus on physician behavior. Along those same lines, Case Western Reserve University has developed a remedial continuing medical education course (Intensive Course in Medical Ethics, Boundaries, and Professionalism) for physicians that was designed in consultation with licensure agencies to address the needs of physicians with problems in the areas of ethics and boundaries.[17] The course includes multiple teaching and assessment methods, such as case discussions, knowledge tests, skills practice, and reflective essays based on the participant's ethical lapse. During a seven-year period from 2005 through 2012 the course had 358 participants.

The University of Colorado School of Medicine recently published results from its comprehensive remediation program[18] that is utilized by medical students, trainees, and attending physicians, with nearly half of participants being medical students. The remediation program is available to learners having a variety of deficits, including deficits in medical knowledge and clinical reasoning and other areas, as well as in professionalism. During a six-year period from 2006 through 2012, 151 learners were referred. An analysis of the program showed that the prevalence of professionalism deficits increased as training level increased. Of note, most learners had more than one deficit. A remediation specialist conducts a semi-structured intake interview with each participant. A "Success Team," comprised of the remediation specialist and learner, and possibly others (e.g., faculty from the referring clerkship, a mental health professional, the student affairs dean), reviews the learner's academic record, direct observations, and other relevant material, and then creates and implements a remediation plan to correct the identified deficit. The plan includes deliberate practice, regular feedback, and an opportunity for the learner to reflect on his or her performance. Reassessments, assigned by the Success Team, are performed by faculty members who are unaware of the learner's remediation status. They may consist of such things as end-of-rotation assessments, direct observations, multiple-choice question exams, or standardized patient encounters. The course, clerkship, or program director receives the results and makes the ultimate determination regarding success of the remediation efforts. Within the University of Colorado program, poor professionalism was the only predictor of probationary status. The program reports an overall remediation success rate of ninety percent, with success meaning that referred learners graduated from their training programs, were in good academic standing, transferred to another program and graduated, or were practicing medicine without restrictions.

While approaches to unprofessional behavior are similar across the continuum of practice from medical student to practicing physician, there are some unique aspects of addressing unprofessionalism at each training level with regard to the types and spectrum of unprofessional behavior, the types of resources that are applicable and available for remediation, and the interventions that are most pertinent to each level of medical training and practice. Focusing specifically on remediation of medical student professionalism, the Ohio State University College of Medicine professionalism program involves a step-wise approach as described below.

Alleged lapses in professionalism may be brought to the attention of any member of the Honor and Professionalism Council (HPC) or directly to the Associate Dean of Student Life. The Associate Dean investigates the concern in order to further characterize the behavior that has occurred. The Associate Dean speaks directly with the reporter (faculty member, resident, or fellow student) and has an exploratory meeting with the accused student to hear his or her viewpoint. Once the Associate Dean determines that the situation merits further evaluation, the case is referred to the Honor and Professionalism Council.

The HPC is comprised of students elected by their class peers, plus a faculty advisor. The HPC holds quarterly business meetings and *ad hoc* hearings. When a student is referred for a professionalism lapse, the HPC assembles a Hearing Committee. The Hearing Committee is comprised of student peers, the faculty advisor, and two non-voting faculty members who contribute input during the hearing. The student meets with the committee and is permitted to bring one individual (advocate) to speak on his or her behalf. During the hearing, the accused student has an opportunity to present his perspective to his peers regarding the behavior that occurred, to provide the context of the situation, and speak to other relevant details. The members of the Hearing Committee seek input from the student to verify the concern, to understand the student's viewpoint, and to learn of any contributing factors. The HPC student members vote to determine whether a lapse has occurred. If the vote affirms that a lapse of professionalism has occurred, the Hearing Committee has an open discussion to formulate a plan of action. The plan is voted on by all members of the Hearing Committee, with a two-thirds majority vote required to approve the recommended remediation plan and a higher majority vote required if the recommendation is for student dismissal. The Associate Dean meets with the student shortly after the hearing to convey the HPC findings and remediation plan.

If the Hearing Committee determines that a professionalism lapse has occurred and that remediation is appropriate, specific interventions and remediation are recommended that are germane to both the individual student and the specific lapse to help the student grow and succeed in his or her professional development. Examples of suggested interventions include assigning the student a faculty mentor or coach, asking the student to prepare a written reflection, asking the student to prepare peer education materials, or referring the student to a specific college or university resource. The Associate Dean of Student Life reviews the HPC remediation plan with the student and implements the plan.

Students who have had a professionalism lapse are followed for any recurrent lapses. It is rare that students return to the HPC for another lapse, either similar or dissimilar, during the remainder of their time in medical school.

Summary and next steps

Several themes emerge from the published literature regarding remediation of professionalism lapses. First, as a medical profession we must maintain self-accountability and adherence to professionalism standards, and we must own and address our shortcomings. Assessment of professional behavior and remediation of lapses should be profession-led and occur across the continuum of practice from the medical student to the trainee to the practicing physician. Efforts to assess and guide professional development need to begin at the earliest stages of medical training.

Remediation programs that address professionalism lapses frequently take a graduated approach, with the intervention matching the severity of the behavior or the recidivism of the offender. Some remediation programs are highly individualized, resource-intensive, and time consuming,[18] which further underscores the need to establish the most effective and efficient practices.

Finally, we need evidence- and outcome-based best methods. Having strategies for remediation of professionalism implies that we are able to identify individuals who are not competent and that remediation is a successful strategy for correcting deficits in professional behavior. Heretofore, there has been a paucity of evidence to guide best practices of remediation in medical education at all levels.[12] To remedy deficiencies in professionalism, physicians and physicians-to-be may need role models, explicit instruction, guided practice, and mentored reflection. Outcome measures that help define the effectiveness of various methods will lead to further refinement of remediation strategies and perhaps to better specificity of methods based on type of behaviors or learning level.

In summary, the medical profession and its individual members must hold itself accountable to standards of competence, ethical values, and interpersonal attributes.[2,3] This call for accountability challenges us to better identify individuals who are not meeting standards of professionalism and to find the best ways to change their behavior.

References

1. Papadakis MA, Paauw DS, Hafferty FW, et al. Perspective: The education community must develop best practices informed by evidence-based research to remediate lapses of professionalism. Acad Med 2012; 87: 1694–98.

2. Wynia MK, Papadakis MA, Sullivan WM, Hafferty FW. More than a list of values and desired behaviors: A foundational understanding of medical professionalism. Acad Med 2014; 89: 712–14.

3. Leach DC. Transcendent professionalism: Keeping promises and living the questions. Acad Med 2014; 89: 699–701.

4. Irby DM, Cooke M, O'Brien BC. Calls for reform of medical education by the Carnegie Foundation for the Advancement of Teaching: 1910 and 2010. Acad Med 2010; 85: 220–27.

5. Bryden P, Ginsburg S, Kurab, B, Ahmed N. Professing professionalism: Are we our own worst enemy? Faculty members' experiences of teaching and evaluating professionalism in medical education at one school. Acad Med 2010; 85: 1025–34.

6. Roff S, Chandratilake M, Mcaleer S, Gibson J. Preliminary benchmarking of appropriate sanctions for lapses in undergraduate professionalism in the health professions. Med Teach 2011; 33: 234–38.

7. Zbieranowski I, Takahashi SG, Verma S, Spadafora SM. Remediation of residents in difficulty: A retrospective 10-year review of the experience of a postgraduate board of examiners. Acad Med 2013; 88: 111–16.

8. Teherani A, O'Sullivan PS, Lovett M, Hauer KE. Categorization of unprofessional behaviours identified during administration of and remediation after a comprehensive clinical performance examination using a validated professionalism framework. Med Teach 2009; 31: 1007–12.

9. Lucey C, Souba W. Perspective: The problem with the problem of professionalism. Acad Med 2010; 85: 1018–24.

10. Cohen JJ. Professionalism in medical education, an American perspective: From evidence to accountability. Med Educ 2006; 40: 607–17.

11. Myers MF, Herb A. Ethical dilemmas in clerkship rotations. Acad Med 2013; 88: 1609–11.

12. Hauer KE, Ciccone A, Henzel TR, et al. Remediation of the deficiencies of physicians across the continuum from medical school to practice: A thematic review of the literature. Acad Med 2009; 84: 1822–32.

13. Buchanan AO, Stallworth J, Christy C, et al. Professionalism in practice: Strategies for assessment, remediation, and promotion. Pediatrics 2012; 129: 407–9.

14. van Mook WN, Gorter SL, De Grave WS, et al. Bad apples spoil the barrel: Addressing unprofessional behaviour. Med Teach 2010; 32: 891–98.

15. Hickson GB, Pichert JW, Webb LE, Gabbe SG. A complementary approach to promoting professionalism: Identifying, measuring, and addressing unprofessional behaviors. Acad Med 2007; 82: 1040–48.

16. Brigham and Women's Hospital. Center for Professionalism and Peer Support. http://www.brighamandwomens.org/medical_professionals/career/cpps/. Accessed May 25, 2014.

17. Parran TV Jr., Pisman AR, Youngner SJ, Levine SB. Evolution of a remedial CME course in professionalism: Addressing learner needs, developing content, and evaluating outcomes. J Contin Educ Health Prof 2013; 33: 174–79.

18. Guerrasio J, Garrity MJ, Aagaard EM. Learner deficits and academic outcomes of medical students, residents, fellows, and attending physicians referred to a remediation program, 2006–2012. Acad Med 2014; 89: 352–58.

Chapter 5
Cultural Transformation in Professionalism
Jo Shapiro, MD

The Center for Professionalism and Peer Support (CPPS) at the Brigham and Women's Hospital (BWH) was founded in 2008, growing out of a sense that a cultural shift within medicine was needed. We were seeing more and more over-worked, stressed physicians facing a steady increase of responsibilities and expectations, often without the resources to support them. We first formulated the Center's mission: to encourage an institutional culture that values and promotes mutual respect, trust, and teamwork. We then developed several core initiatives to support our mission. These include: peer support following adverse events, unanticipated outcomes, or other emotionally stressful events such as caring for trauma victims; disclosure coaching; defendant support; teamwork and effective communication training; wellness programs; and a professionalism initiative. Our professionalism initiative[1] is the focus of this chapter. We feel strongly, however, that the support and training offered through all of our programs is central to enhancing a supportive and cohesive professional culture within our institution.

Changing institutional culture is a lofty goal. We approach this challenge with the understanding that the culture of an institution is something that we define and redefine every day. It is not primarily about what is written in a policy or a code of conduct. While those things can be vitally important, we recognize that the culture of our workplaces is organic and is expressed daily though our actions and values. To make meaningful culture change we need to be present and active with both support for and education around professional behavior.

Professionalism education and training

We define professionalism as behavior that helps build trustworthy relationships. This means all relationships—between a clinician and patient, a physician and nurse, any health care team member and a student—are important.

In building our professionalism initiative, we understood the importance of setting expectations as well as providing education and training. In order to raise awareness about behavioral expectations as well as about our training and support efforts, every physician at BWH from intern through senior faculty is required to participate in our interactive simulation-based professionalism training sessions. We partnered with Employment Learning Innovations (ELI), an employment law company, to design the curriculum using video scenarios with an accompanying workbook.

One of the video vignettes features Dr. Mills—a well meaning (we assume) surgeon who finds himself significantly under-resourced. We have all had moments when we feel highly stressed for multiple possible reasons such as having to be in two places at once, feeling as if those around us are under-performing, needing lab results that are unavailable, or not having access to important patient information. This is where Dr. Mills finds himself, and he behaves in a way that seems completely inexcusable and horrendous. During the session participants identify the disruptive behaviors being exhibited—what specifically Dr. Mills did that was unprofessional—and we talk about how he could have handled the situation differently. In addition, we role play giving Dr. Mills feedback about his behavior. In facilitating these discussions we acknowledge that it's very easy to sit in any training session and believe that we ourselves would never behave in this unprofessional way; we point out that most of us are, in fact, capable of this kind of behavior. Given a situation with stressors such as poor resources, sleep deprivation, or overwhelming responsibility, most of us are at risk of behaving somewhat—or even completely—unprofessionally.

These professionalism sessions are just the beginning of an institutional conversation. Our Center has other resources for ongoing professional development, such as training in conflict and stress management as well as workshops to help clinicians develop skills in giving feedback.

In addition, we emphasize that when interacting with a colleague who is exhibiting disruptive behavior, there are other options beyond reporting the behavior. Ideally, we'd like to be training people to address bad behavior when they see it—to have a clear and respectful conversation with the person about the behavior at issue. Yet we recognize that in a hierarchical environment it will not always be or feel safe to have these direct conversations; we therefore must have a process in which people can come forward and voice their concerns. While our institution has a hierarchy of responsibility, we do not have a hierarchy of respect: we are all equal when it comes to deserving respect.

Handling professionalism concerns

We cannot expect people to behave respectfully or feel supported in a culture that does not hold people accountable for their behavior. If anyone has a concern about a physician's unprofessional behavior at our institution—the person with the concern (the reporter) can be a student, nurse, secretary, faculty member—that person can address the concern through the Center. We first meet with the reporter to listen, discuss, and decide together on a plan. One of our guiding principles in handling these concerns includes being as discreet and respectful as possible to everyone, including the person about whom the concerns are reported (the focus person).

As a next step we generally like to speak with other people who work with the focus person, and we make sure that the reporter is comfortable with our doing that. We explain that this inquiry is not a 360° evaluation—this is a very important point. We are specifically investigating one aspect of someone's professional behavior. If the reporter agrees, we solicit the names of people he or she recommends, and we then perform multisource interviews. We assure the reporter and the people we contact subsequently that we have a safe system that focuses on the specific problematic behavior. We gather data and then bring this information to the focus person's supervisory physician, such as a chief or chair, to get his or her perspective.

How the supervisor responds is variable and determines our next steps. Sometimes he or she is well aware of the problem but has not taken any action to remediate it. Generally the supervisor does not know how to address the problem. It stands to reason that supervisors have had trouble giving the focus person feedback in the past, as few leaders have had training in giving difficult feedback. We then agree on a plan that generally involves our meeting with the focus person together. This meeting accomplishes two things. First, it provides on-the-job training for the chair or chief to see how to conduct these difficult feedback conversations. Second, the focus person responds differently when his or her supervisor is there to support the importance of having this conversation and of holding the person accountable for his or her behavior. A critical point that we stress in this conversation is the unacceptability of any retaliatory behavior on the part of the focus person.

We have developed an algorithm for giving frame-based feedback[2] that provides the basic format for this meeting with the focus person. First we state the specific types of behavioral concerns. It is important to remind the focus person that this is not a performance evaluation. We are not suggesting that this problematic behavior is all that defines the person's career. After clearly stating the specific problematic behaviors and why they are concerning, the second step of the algorithm is to elicit the focus person's frame—how she or he understands the problem. The third step of the algorithm is to match the discussion to the focus person's frame.

The central tenet of this feedback technique involves using the principles of autonomy support—having the person tap into his or her intrinsic motivation to change behavior. We may try to draw out the focus person's empathy by saying something like: "This is how many people feel when they work with you. Did you know that this is the impact your actions have on your team?" Sometimes this leads to a discussion of systems issues that the person feels are contributing to his or her behavior patterns. We communicate clearly that we do understand the difficulties, but that these do not obviate personal accountability for the behavior. This is not to say that systems issues are not real or contributory, and we do not ignore them when they are. We have to be willing to advocate for people in addressing systems changes, but at the same time people need to understand that they still must behave respectfully despite real situational challenges.

The focus person might, alternatively, frame his or her angry or disparaging behavior as trying to get better patient care. In fact one of the most frequent reactions to a discussion of unprofessional behavior is: "I am a patient advocate and I need to behave this way in order to protect my patient." We respond to this by explaining that we understand and respect that commitment to patient care, and we recognize the person's reputation for being a patient advocate. We point out that what the person likely doesn't realize is the correlation between unprofessional behavior, problematic teamwork communication, and negative patient outcomes. We explain that the individual's behavior actually puts patients at risk; that this is a safety issue. We explore the fact that the impact of that negative behavior is in direct opposition to the person's intent. This is an example of how we match the discussion to the focus person's frame as a way to encourage intrinsic motivation for behavior change.

Another example of matching the discussion to the focus person's frame is when the behavior in question involves sexual harassment. Sometimes the person's response is defensive, denying responsibility. For example, the focus person might explain why the behavior has nothing to do with him or her; he or she explains that it is really about someone trying to retaliate for an unfairly perceived slight. We respond by explaining that regardless of why the person thinks the behavior was reported, the important point is that the behavior can never happen again. We will then send the focus person to outside counsel for a discussion of the extensive legal trouble that can result if the behavior continues. This approach generally motivates behavior change.

With this same complaint, a different response we may see is embarrassment and apology. The person thought he was being friendly; his frame might be that he was simply making a clumsy attempt at connecting with a colleague. Yet upon reflection, he understands why the behavior is unacceptable. Our response to this frame is quite different from our response to the person who does not accept responsibility. To this person we explain that while we do understand his intent, the behavior made a colleague very uncomfortable. This level of discussion and intervention is generally enough to correct the problem; outside counsel is used just to reinforce the legal ramifications.

One challenge in giving difficult feedback is the unpredictability of people's reactions and the reality that we cannot control these reactions. The challenge is to work with whatever comes up and be flexible in the response, depending on the focus person's frame. Our process is therefore both generally consistent and completely personal, depending on the person's frame and reactions to the feedback. In responding, we also must take into account how egregious the behavior is and how long it has been going on.

These examples demonstrate that we hear a somewhat familiar pattern of responses from people when giving feedback. Regardless of whether the focus person has personal insight, our job is to explain that that person must change his or her behavior if he or she wants to stay at our institution. This must be the bottom line. The person does not have to agree; our job then becomes managing people who do not recognize the importance of changing their behavior.

Most importantly, we all must be held equally accountable. Not holding everyone to the same behavioral expectations allows for a double standard that can be more damaging than doing nothing at all. Our accountability process is, among other things, designed to address egregious or repetitive unprofessional behavior. Without remediating this kind of behavior we cannot take our work to the next level—working to promote healthy team dynamics and helping individuals communicate effectively with one another. The reality is that there simply are some workplace bullies—people who do not respond to feedback and do not recognize the destructive effects of their own behaviors. These people—a small minority—tend to only respond and begin to change when they are threatened with external consequences such as losing their positions. When presented with the need to change their behavior some people refuse to accept personal responsibility; they respond with denial, anger, and threats that can be extremely demoralizing and damaging to an institution's professional culture. This is why our process must account for both types of individuals. In order to feel confident that our program could manage the full spectrum of problematic behavior it was, and still remains, critical that we have the unwavering support and backing of our institutional leadership. Dr. Gary Gottlieb, BWH President at the time of the Center's founding, as well as our current President, Dr. Elizabeth Nabel, have been unequivocal in their commitment to stand behind our work.

Our work with the focus person is entirely behavior-based. We have learned not to go down the rabbit hole of trying too hard to understand the potential reasons for the person's behavior. For example, we do not explore the possibility that the person has a personality disorder or should be evaluated. We found, early on in this work, that this approach resulted in significant distraction from the real issue at hand, and we found ourselves over-referring in an attempt to diagnose the reason behind the behavior. As a result, we have shifted toward a focus on the behavior itself and away from attempting to diagnose. This is not to say that we don't offer people resources, because we do. And if we find that someone is impaired, this is a different matter: in these cases we are very quick to refer them to Physician Health Services, an outside professional group that evaluates physicians for impairment. But we are much more frequently called in to address repetitive unprofessional behaviors without an obvious underlying behavioral health issue.

Another area of caution, in addition to being careful not to "treat" the focus person as we might a patient, is the concept of cultural relativism. People sometimes point to cultural excuses or explanations for their unprofessional behavior. Our response is quite clear—it's not relevant that this behavior is tolerated elsewhere; you cannot behave that way here. We describe the problematic behavior to the focus person, explain that the behavior needs to stop, and describe the behavior we expect going forward.

One of the biggest barriers we face in this work is, interestingly, too high a tolerance on the part of supervisory physicians. They may be overly concerned about the focus person's career; all they can see is a colleague whom they hired and have devoted considerable time and energy into helping develop. As a result, there are times when we at CPPS are "holding" all of the damage and sadness that results from this bad behavior. Our role at that point is to help the supervisor understand the degree of destruction caused by the unprofessional behavior. In this way, the suffering of those people impacted by the unprofessional behavior is made visible to the leadership. We do this with the important support of our chief medical officer (CMO) Stan Ashley, MD, as well as our legal counsel for the hospital, Joan Stoddard. Sometimes in particularly intractable situations it can make all the difference to have the CMO in the room to support our process. We have also formed a professionalism advisory committee that meets quarterly to review cases. At the end of the day, this cultural transformation can only happen with strong institutional support.

Outcomes

Since 2009 we have had 270 individual physicians about whom concerns were raised (and there may have been more than one concern per person) and ten instances of our assisting with team dysfunction. We categorize the problematic behavior broadly as follows: demeaning, angry, uncollegial, shirking responsibilities, hypercritical, unprofessional patient communications, clinical dyscompetence, misconduct, and sexual harassment.

One of the central tenets of this process, and what makes it functional and useful, is that we all must be held accountable. Our goal is not to get rid of people; our goal is to motivate them to change their behavior. Yet we must, at the same time, demonstrate the accountability of this process in our insistence that physicians with repeated and egregious unprofessional behavior cannot remain at BWH. Since 2009, twenty-five physicians have left BWH due to professionalism concerns, and six were demoted from positions of authority.

Support programs

We recognize that while holding each other accountable, we also need to support one another. People perform best in a supportive environment. We therefore have developed programs in which we have physician and nurse peers reach out to clinicians in times of emotional distress, such as being involved in an adverse event or when facing a lawsuit. The trained peers are there to listen, empathize, and offer suggestions for healing and recovery. One study we performed showed that ninety percent of physicians wanted to talk to a physician colleague, not a mental health professional, after an adverse event.[3] If a physician needs to make a disclosure to a patient, we have disclosure coaches who work with risk management to help the physician prepare to have compassionate and transparent conversations with the patient and family, and who also understand the emotional challenges facing the physician.

Conclusion

In this context of supporting and being there for each other, we believe that our professionalism initiative and other support programs are all necessary and beneficial elements of the positive change we seek to make within the institution. Culture is manifested by how we speak to each other, our ability to encourage staff to speak up when someone is not behaving well, and what we do to support one another. Our support and accountability programs demonstrate that the institution values and respects its employees. I will end with a quote from Vaclav Havel about hope, which he believes is "not the conviction that something will turn out well, but the certainty that something makes sense, regardless of how it turns out. The hope of fellowship, and kindness, and service."

Acknowledgment
I would like to thank Pamela Galowitz for her invaluable help in editing this chapter.

References
1. Shapiro J, Whittemore AW, Tsen LC. Instituting a culture of professionalism:

The establishment of a center for professionalism and peer support. Jt Comm J Qual Patient Saf 2014; 40: 168–77.

2. Rudolph J, Raemer D, Shapiro J. We know what they did wrong, but not why: The case for "frame-based" feedback. Clin Teach 2013; 10: 186–89.

3. Hu YY, Fix ML. Hevelone ND, Lipsitz SR, et al. Physicians' needs in coping with emotional stressors: The case for peer support. Arch Surg 2012; 147: 212–17.

Chapter 6

Enhancing Interprofessional Professionalism: A Systems Approach

Rebecca Saavedra, EdD

The University of Texas Medical Branch (UTMB) has a long-standing commitment to promoting interprofessional professionalism (IPP). A 2007 *Academic Medicine* article, "The Journey to Creating a Campus-Wide Culture of Professionalism,"[1] described our philosophy, definitions, and initiatives to instill professionalism that began over a decade before. Since then our professionalism endeavors and understanding of interprofessionalism have continued to evolve. Today we recognize the significance of IPP as a strategic priority and component of not only our institution's success but key to better integrated care outcomes. This paper bridges what was initially undertaken as a campus-wide interdisciplinary professionalism effort with our current understanding and emphasis on interprofessional practice.

UTMB's campus-wide approach to interdisciplinary collaboration was undertaken to link all members of the university community to the principles and behaviors focused on patient-, family-, and client-centered care. Today's brave new world of health care is altering practice and relationships so significantly that in the near term academic health centers (AHCs) will need to have fully transformed into new collaborative partnerships among practitioners, patients, and their families. The "core of professionalism" involves "those attitudes and behaviors that serve to maintain patient interest above physician self-interest."[2] These principles remain fundamental and timeless but with a freshly imbued sense of urgency and inclusiveness.

Once the concern was that the coming changes in the health care delivery system would "reduce the status of patients to commodities" and "have a negative impact on the professional behavior of physicians."[2] Today we understand that AHCs must address environmental challenges that require integrated care models, better outcomes, lower costs, and enhanced patient satisfaction. The emphasis on new models of care relies on collaborative effective interprofessional teams as a strategic foundation to achieve a patient-centered organization that fully engages patients in their care. IPP is no longer an ideal; it is a pragmatic reality.

Over the past almost two decades, UTMB has established a systematic mix of programs—clinical- and academic-based—to meet the new challenges and adapt in a dynamic health care environment. UTMB's systems approach instills a focus on action to promote interprofessionalism across the institution for students, faculty, and employees. These processes are aimed at understanding, influencing, monitoring, and adjusting our efforts based on experience and lessons learned to accelerate our progress toward a more interdependent professional environment. This approach builds in opportunities for dialogue, evaluation, and improvement, thus allowing for organizational transformation. The organizational vision is set by executive leadership whose actions demonstrate their commitment and systematic focus on professionalism as a standard of conduct for everyone at UTMB. As the UTMB Professionalism Charter states: "The foundation for UTMB's culture of professionalism is rooted in the trust placed in those who deliver patient care, conduct research, educate future health care professionals, provide administrative support, maintain a supportive environment and strive to learn."[3]

The transformation begins

Establishing a culture of IPP can only succeed if there is critical leadership sponsorship and an infrastructure in place to ensure that policies and systems support skilled practitioners who work respectfully and collaboratively in effective teams. The UTMB Professionalism initiative has been in place continuously since 1998, spanning two university presidencies to the present. UTMB Presidential sponsorship is indispensable in not only guaranteeing necessary resources but also in elevating activities to institutional prominence.

Additional strategic partnerships have been forged with the Provost/ Dean of Medicine; Deans of Health Professions, Nursing and Graduate Schools; CEO of the Health System; and the Executive Vice President of Business and Finance. These individuals serve as members of the President's Executive Committee and set the tone of collaboration and respect across the institution. The Executive Committee is a critical ally in crafting and delivering the message to the various segments of the campus community.

Over time, UTMB has established a matrix of institutional programs, initiatives, and monitoring systems to create a focus on action and engagement by the campus community to form a collegial and patient-centered environment. Early on, discussion forums were held to define and reflect on the concept's meaning across disciplines. Meetings with department chairs, faculty senate, and student senate were a part of a "listening tour" to determine the readiness of the campus culture to adopt a multidisciplinary perspective. The outcome underscored that what unites the education, research, and patient care missions of the organization is a patient-centered focus and that professionalism is a collective obligation.

In the beginning, the university's IPP philosophy was not embraced by all members of the campus community. Bridging differences and rejecting an entitlement mentality were essential to merge individual and discipline expertise into a common multidisciplinary understanding. The strategy focused on the mutual goal of improved treatment outcomes and patient care, de-emphasizing competition and accentuating a shared vision of high functioning teams.

The professionalism committee instrument for change

In 1998 the UTMB Professionalism Board was formed to develop a multidisciplinary approach to advancing professionalism, recognizing that a fundamental concern for the patient should characterize all members of the AHC community. The Board's charge was to launch a comprehensive set of professionalism initiatives throughout the institution and to transform the culture of health care training and practice.

The Board has evolved over time to become the Professionalism Committee, and has played a central role in executing and linking key professionalism initiatives. It has met continuously since 1998, proactively addressing campus issues and changes in the health care delivery system that impact professional behavior and the healing environment. The Committee regularly monitors results of institutional climate surveys, and meets with the President, Provost, Deans, and Student Government to proactively address ethical challenges and provide recommendations and seek action as needed.

Membership continues to include individuals from across the mission areas and workforce segments (e.g., academic and health system administration, physicians, nurses, faculty, and students from all four UTMB schools). The broad representation ensures that messages can be tailored to suit respective points of view. Members are appointed by the President and have demonstrated a commitment to professionalism and, because of each member's specific role, serve as knowledgeable and effective change agents.

Given the diversity and breadth of roles, the committee is able to address matters related to IPP across the enterprise and to recommend and influence solutions in the academic and clinical arena. Four of its members have attended the highly recognized Vanderbilt University Disruptive Behavior Conference and provide valued insight and direction. In addition, UTMB has within its ranks recognized leaders in the field of professionalism, professional identity formation, and bioethics. These experts provide invaluable guidance to the institution and committee.

Putting the charter into practice

Starting in 2000 a series of university programs were developed to build awareness about exemplary models of professional behavior. These included: Going the Extra Mile, a campus-wide program for staff, students, and faculty to recognize outstanding professional qualities of their peers; the John P. McGovern Academy of Oslerian Medicine, which endows School of Medicine faculty who exemplify ideals of professionalism and humanism; and You Count employee surveys to solicit perceptions about workforce culture.

In 2002, the effort to define professionalism on campus gained momentum with the publication of the Physician Charter in the *Annals of Internal Medicine*[4] and *Lancet*,[5] which identified and defined the principles and commitments of professionalism. With a grant from the American Board of Internal Medicine, UTMB began to explore the Physician Charter's application to the university. The result is the UTMB Professionalism Charter,[3] which extends the professionalism themes and standards of conduct to everyone at UTMB—faculty, staff, and students.

The university's position was pioneering and has proven to be an important strategy to address the critical success factors in today's academic health systems. Health care's future is systems-based and embraces team-based practice to improve clinical outcomes and effective care coordination. The core of these relationships is interprofessionalism, focused on greater collaboration, respect, and effective communication.

The UTMB Charter was written with this integrative model in mind to encompass the campus as a whole, recognizing that all members of the AHC community share equal responsibility for its professional commitments, "from the clinician who ensures quality care, to the staff member who ensures confidentiality of patient records."[1] The Charter's mandate therefore is to hold every member of the UTMB community accountable for acting with integrity, compassion and respect towards one another and those we serve.[3]

The UTMB Professionalism Charter is a living document that is regularly reviewed and updated. The Charter serves as a capstone for all discipline-specific standards and codes of conduct. It is a unifying set of beliefs and behaviors that are professed to the community. The ten commitments have been written so that a "line of sight" is meaningful from wherever in the institution one stands or whatever role one has. "Everyone who works or studies at the University of Texas Medical Branch is a member of a community of professionals dedicated to advancing UTMB's mission, vision and values."[3] The Professionalism Charter is utilized in our orientation and leadership programs. All fundamental efforts to improve the capability and capacity of our workforce are inextricably linked to the standards outlined in the Charter.

The Charter's main objective is to build strong understanding and consensus, while generating a culture that allows and encourages dialogue that is both candid and meaningful.

UTMB Professionalism Charter Commitments

1. Commitment to a culture of trust
2. Commitment to diversity
3. Commitment to competence and growth
4. Commitment to confidentiality
5. Commitment to honesty
6. Commitment to the responsible use of resources
7. Commitment to value
8. Commitment to appropriate relations
9. Commitment to manage conflicts of interest
10. Commitment to the appropriate discovery and use of knowledge

Honor pledge

While the UTMB Charter was being developed another IPP endeavor was occurring across campus. It is important to acknowledge the role students played in the progression of IPP at UTMB. Their passion, compassion, and altruism were a source of vitality to the movement. It began with efforts of the Medical School Student Honor Education Council, which saw a need to educate and address academic integrity issues that were driven from students' perspective and yet complementary to institutional efforts. The students' close association with other health professions student organizations quickly resulted in IPP becoming a multidisciplinary effort and the development of a four-school unifying statement of IPP.

> On my honor, as a member of the UTMB community, I pledge to act with integrity, compassion, and respect in all my academic and professionalism endeavors.

Each word was deliberated at length, with students and faculty reflecting on the values that are inherent in the various codes of conduct and standards of the health professions. The honor pledge encapsulates the key values of IPP. It is a measure of the professional and academic evaluation of students in all courses and complements the UTMB Student Conduct and Discipline Policy.

Honor pledge plaques and signs are displayed throughout UTMB, serving as a reminder of the basic principles. The pledge is introduced to new students at the All School Orientation and New Student Welcome events, which themselves are examples of UTMB's interprofessional tradition.

The orientation includes new students from each of the four schools and includes a Welcome Weekend of team building and networking activities. The program is a collaborative university event that is hosted by passionate volunteers of second-year students from all four schools, faculty, and staff who serve as facilitators and staff. The All School Orientation and Welcome Weekend showcase UTMB values and mission and set expectations that students are members of a diverse community of professionals who share a common set of professional values.

Becoming a professional

UTMB also has augmented student development activities with formal course work to engrain professionalism and interprofessionalism throughout the curriculum of the four schools. For example, the Graduate School of Biomedical Sciences convenes an annual seminar on ethics of scientific research, the School of Nursing has classes on ethical practice and cultural sensitivity, and the School of Health Professions and School of Medicine (SOM) have embedded professionalism in the students' training and curriculum.

In 2005, the SOM introduced professionalism with five longitudinal themes across the medical curriculum to ensure broad integration with medical training. During the first and second years, the practice of medicine course[6] engages students in small group discussions about health care delivery, interprofessional teamwork, and ethical practice. The sessions encourage opportunities for reflective growth. The faculty continues to seek opportunities to enhance the professionalism themes within existing and new classes, programs, and activities.

UTMB has implemented an Interprofessional Education program with courses open to all students for credit. These include: Foundations in Patient Safety and Health Care Quality; Spirituality and Clinical Care; and Global Health Interprofessional Core Course. An Interprofessional Pediatric Advocacy Program is designed to have students work in interprofessional teams with Child Protective Services caseworkers and families. Pediatric End-of-Life Simulation brings students together from all of the schools to participate in a high-fidelity simulation focused on the care of an infant and family as a child faces cardiopulmonary arrest. Annually, UTMB hosts Interprofessional Education Day, which features a keynote speaker and a series of simulation workshops involving interprofessional teams of students with a trained facilitator.

UTMB has augmented the curriculum with experiential opportunities for interprofessional teamwork through intentional student community service learning projects.[7] Frontera de Salud and St. Vincent's Free Clinic are student-run community service projects that were founded and staffed by medicine, nursing, and health professions students to provide community-based health programs. Both student organizations promote opportunities for our students to work with interprofessional teams. Our students' evaluations of these experiences continue to be positive year after year.

"Do as you say, not as you do"

Jordan Cohen, president emeritus of the Association of American Medical Colleges states, "Unless we convert our learning environments from crucibles of cynicism into cradles of professionalism, no amount of effort in the admission arena is going to suffice."[8] Bullying behavior is inimical to interprofessional professionalism. Verbal and physical harassment and intimidation are unfortunate standard examples of mistreatment endured by health care learners operating through informal clinical and classroom interactions forming what is known as the hidden curriculum.[9] On July 9, 2008, the Joint Commission published the Sentinel Event Alert, Issue 40, that declares, "Intimidating and disruptive behaviors can foster medical errors, contribute to poor patient satisfaction and to preventable adverse outcomes, increase the cost of care and cause qualified clinicians, administrators and managers to seek new positions in more professional environments."[10]

UTMB is committed to providing the best educational climate possible and recognizes the need to safeguard students who may be the victims of or witnesses to unprofessional and disruptive behavior by faculty. The inherent vulnerability of students and their dread of reprisal may leave them reluctant to protest such behavior. In 2004, UTMB introduced an online mechanism for students to report unprofessional behavior or mistreatment—whether from a resident, faculty member, fellow student, or staff.

The Professionalism Concern Report (PCR) is located prominently on the UTMB Professionalism website and allows students from all four schools to bring forward professionalism concerns to a neutral third party. The forms can be submitted anonymously by students; they may also meet with the Student Ombudsman or other officials as an option. The PCR is triaged by the co-chairs of the Professionalism Committee (a SOM faculty and a university administrator) and sent to the appropriate department chair/manager to resolve the student concern.

Examples of unprofessional behaviors reported include: verbal abuse, public belittlement, disparaging comments by faculty or other health care team members, discourtesy in the classroom by fellow students, or student cheating. The administrator is asked to address the issue by following up with the faculty, student, or employee within his or her department.

The action begins by a determination of what events can be validated. A conversation with the faculty or staff member is convened and then appropriate action is taken. The action might be as modest as a brief conversation and a verbal reminder of appropriate standards of conduct and behavior. With serious findings a more directive action plan might be the outcome. The intention of this process is to remind and remediate. Faculty and other members of the UTMB community have a responsibility to be accountable to one another and immediately address lapses in behavior and support the remediation of problems. Being accountable constitutes the essence of professional behavior.

Remediating student professionalism

Campus-wide remediation and intervention mechanisms have been introduced to address student professionalism. At UTMB, faculty and staff have an opportunity to assess student professionalism as a part of students' academic evaluation across the four years. If faculty or staff observe behavior that is inappropriate by a student they may submit an Early Concern Note (ECN) for follow up action. The ECN is an informal intervention process that is separate from the academic record.

"[ECN] is a part of a campus wide initiative to heighten awareness of the importance of professionalism behavior."[11] It remains confidential between the student and the Associate Dean, unless and until a student receives three or more ECNs during matriculation. It is not anonymous and students receive a copy of the report as a part of the mentoring and guidance process. Some student behaviors, such as academic dishonesty and unlawful behavior, are not a part of this process and are administered through the Student Affairs office as a part of the University Conduct and Discipline Policy. The ECN is not punitive, but allows for unprofessional actions to be addressed quickly and may reveal patterns of behaviors that could advance to truly significant concerns over time.

Monitoring climate

Because UTMB undertook its professionalism initiative enterprise-wide to ensure an interdisciplinary approach, the initiative has utilized multiple modalities to promote and measure its program effectiveness. UTMB conducts a series of student, employee, and patient surveys to measure effectiveness of programs and activities that enable a professional environment. The student survey contains a series of questions that asks respondents to reflect and assess the institution's commitment to professionalism and interprofessionalism, to faculty's commitment to maintaining respectful professional relationships, and to the extent to which one has observed faculty and students modeling the Charter commitments.

Student satisfaction scores (from all schools) over three years (2011 through 2013) have overall sustained high marks, with recent slightly negative declines in some areas. For example, after several years (2002 through 2007) of positive gains, in 2007 96% of students rated professionalism as a priority at UTMB; in 2013, 95% of students from all four schools reported that professionalism is a priority at UTMB. In 2007, 93% students reported that they had been treated with courtesy and respect by faculty. In 2011, 92% of students reported that they had been treated with courtesy and respect by faculty; in 2013, the rate revealed a small decline to 89%.

The scores also decline slightly when the students are asked to assess their cohort's professionalism. In 2011, 86% all students reported that students are courteous and respectful in the classroom; in 2013, it had fallen slightly to 83%. In 2011, 89% students indicated that "cheating is not a problem at UTMB"; in 2013 the score had changed to 87%. Survey written responses and forums with students and faculty have identified environmental, demographic, and technological disruptors that have provoked adverse outcomes.

In 2011, UTMB began to survey students about their interprofessionalism experiences. In 2011, 79% of all students reported "While at UTMB I have developed an appreciation for the value of inter-professional teamwork"; in 2013, it has risen slightly to 81%. The same holds true for "While at UTMB, I have learned about the role of different health care professions" (2011 82%; 2013 83%) and "I have had an opportunity to participate in inter-professional activities" (2011 77%; 2013 86%).

UTMB conducts an employee satisfaction survey regularly to measure workforce climate. The survey asks employees to assess "The person I report to treats me with respect" and "UTMB treats employees with respect. In 2011 using a Likert scale of 1 = strongly disagree to 5 = strongly agree, the responses were 4.25 and 3.72 respectively; in 2012, 4.23 and 3.70 respectively, and in 2013, 4.22 and 3.67 respectively. These responses have trended down slightly.

Monitoring and measuring professionalism and interprofessionalism outcomes are crucial to understanding institutional performance and avenues of improvement. Results from various student, patient, and workforce surveys indicate that progress continues to be made, but that we have not achieved our objective. Senior leaders utilize survey and quality data to initiate two-way communication, reinforce behavior, and improve performance. A focus on behavioral aspects of performance and interpersonal relationships complements institutional quality initiatives and strategic objectives.

Advancing IPP during a stable environment is problematic; attempting to improve interprofessional collaboration, communication, and respect during turbulent financial and environmental conditions is even more difficult. Health care reform, financial challenges, consumerism, and value-based purchasing are just a few of the changing environmental forces impacting education, research, and health care. Reviewing survey results allows us to gauge our success, improve our knowledge, and address opportunities for continuous improvement. The slight downturn in performance has resulted in the organization developing action plans, deploying additional targeted "pulse surveys," and increased communication between learners and faculty and employees and managers to determine the root cause of issues. UTMB is approaching the challenge as an opportunity to role model transparency and collaboration among its leaders.

The assessment tools enumerated above reflect only a small part of UTMB's effort to measure the impact of professionalism and interprofessional activities. UTMB is committed to maintaining high standards of excellence, integrity, and accountability, whether it involves academic or research activities, clinical practice, or institutional decision-making by faculty and employees.

Promoting professionalism

UTMB hosts a Professionalism Summit biennially to address the pedagogy of professionalism and the importance of addressing unprofessional behaviors. The speakers list is a who's who in the field of professionalism. In 2004, Maxine Papadakis, MD, lectured on the association between unprofessional behavior among medical students and subsequent disciplinary action by state medical boards.[12] Her pioneering work was foundational in UTMB's development of the Early Concern Note process. In 2009, David Leach, MD, presented on "Creating a Culture of Professionalism: Reconnecting Soul and Role. In 2011 and 2012, Gerald Hickson, MD, presented "A Complementary Approach to Professionalism: Identifying, Measuring and Addressing Unprofessional Behaviors" and "Dealing with Behaviors that Undermine a Culture of Safety." Dr. Hickson's presentations engaged clinical chairs and health system leadership in a critical dialogue on the importance of proactively addressing disruptive behaviors.[13] In 2014, Barbara Balik, RN, MS, PhD, delivered "Interprofessionalism—Why Bother?" Dr. Balik's session emphasized the impact and attributes of a high functioning team.

These presentations were instrumental in guiding and informing our journey and provided an opportunity to listen and interact with innovative national experts in the field. The insights gained ignited candid debates about the hidden curriculum, self-regulation, and the strategic challenges AHCs are facing. Annually UTMB hosts either the biennial Summit or informal "brown bag" workshops. These events are powerful reminders about our responsibility as role models and about the obligation to speak out and engage those who act unprofessionally.

Interprofessional professionalism as a strategic objective

Professionalism is recognized as critical to the organization's future success. The Professionalism Charter's mandate to "hold every member of the UTMB community accountable for acting with integrity, compassion and respect toward one another and those we serve" is one of the institutional strategic goals. UTMB has deployed systematic approaches to develop and assess workforce engagement and climate. High performance is characterized by effective communication, patient/client/student focus, knowledge, skills, and respectful behaviors. Transforming our internal relationships requires proactive intentional processes put in place to reinforce professional values and ethical business practices.

IPP is more than a theoretical concept or an ideal; it is a strategic imperative and core competency of today's AHC. Societal, economic, and technological innovations are disrupting not only traditional hierarchical structures and relationships among health professionals, but the relationships between provider and patient as well. Innovative training and IPP education can provide health professionals with opportunities to gain the skills, knowledge, attitudes, and behaviors needed to fully participate in integrative health care delivery systems.

UTMB's model for interprofessional professionalism

Promoting IPP is a multifaceted endeavor and requires a supportive infrastructure, leadership engagement, and strategic foresight to recognize the fundamental pressures effecting change at AHCs. It requires a matrix of policies, processes, and individuals committed to addressing unprofessional behaviors that negatively impact the team's performance and patient outcomes. Significantly, it requires the passion and cooperation of faculty members who serve on the front line as health providers, colleagues, and teachers. As Hickson and colleagues note, "Every physician needs skills for conducting informal interventions with peers."[13] It is critical that faculty, residents, and senior leaders provide appropriate models of respect and inspire each other to act with integrity, compassion, and respect. Role models must be recognized, nurtured, and valued.

UTMB has implemented a comprehensive program to sustain professional behavior and enhance interprofessionalism. Strong leadership focus and a systems approach have shaped a culture of shared values and inter-disciplinary collaboration at UTMB for fifteen years. The professionalism initiative is still on course with critical lessons learned and continued emphasis on sustaining an interprofessional professionalism culture:

1. A reporting mechanism and clear policies are important to support the vulnerable members of the community and hold the individuals accountable.

2. A vigilant effort is needed that promotes and continually reminds community members of the values and behaviors that are shared by all.

3. Leadership and management training is necessary to provide skills to address poor performance and disruptive behaviors.

4. Annual performance evaluation and satisfaction surveys must be deployed and results measured to effect change.

5. Recognition that professionalism is a strategic objective that is foundational; it signifies the importance of civility and respect to other members of the health care team.

6. AHCs are at a crossroads that demand an integrated and collaborative vision to improve interdisciplinary collaboration and professionalism in a patient-centered integrated-care environment. What will not change over time is a commitment to patients' welfare, the duty to uphold scientific standards, and the importance of respectful engagement by all disciplines.

UTMB has developed a systems approach to address and sustain its commitment to professionalism and interprofessionalism. This strategy elevates the primacy of professional and ethical behavior and demands it as a core competency critical to the organization's mission.

Professionalism is the standard of conduct for everyone at UTMB with a clear recognition that everyone at UTMB is a member of a community of professionals and it takes everyone to advance the university's mission, vision, and values.

References

1. Smith KL, Saavedra R, Raeke J, O'Donell AA. The journey to creating a campus-wide culture of professionalism. Acad Med 2007; 82: 1015–21.

2. American Board of Internal Medicine. Project Professionalism. Philadelphia (PA): American Board of Internal Medicine. Available at http://www.abimfoundation.org/Resource-Center/Bibliography/~/media/Files/Resource%20Center/Project%20professionalism.ashx.

3. University of Texas Medical Branch. UTMB Professionalism Charter. Available at http://www.utmb.edu/professionalism/about-us/professionalism-charter.aspx.

4. ABIM Foundation, American Board of Internal Medicine; ACP-ASIM

Foundation, American College of Physicians-American Society of Internal Medicine; European Federation of Internal Medicine. Medical professionalism in the new millennium: A physician charter. Ann Intern Med 2002; 136: 243–46.

5. Medical Professionalism Project. Medical professionalism in the new millennium: A physician's charter. Lancet 2002; 359: 520–22.

6. University of Texas Medical Branch School of Medicine. Course Information: Year 2 Practice of Medicine. http://www.utmb.edu/imo/courses/year2/pom2.asp.

7. Muller D, Meah Y, Griffith J, et al. The role of social and community service in medical education: The next 100 years. Acad Med 2010; 85: 302–09.

8. Cohen J. Our compact with tomorrow's doctors. Acad Med 2002; 77: 475–80.

9. Hafferty FW, Franks R. The hidden curriculum, ethics teaching, and the structure of medical education. Acad Med 1994; 69: 861–71.

10. The Joint Commission. Sentinel Event Alert. Issue 40, July 9, 2008 Available at: http://www.jointcommission.org/assets/1/18/SEA_40.pdf.

11. Ainsworth MA, Szauter KM. Medical student professionalism: Are we measuring the right behaviors? A comparison of professional lapses by students and physicians. Acad Med 2006; 81 (10 Suppl.): S83–86.

12. Papadakis MA, Hodgson CS, Teherani A, Kohatsu ND. Unprofessional behavior in medical school is associated with subsequent disciplinary action by a state medical board. Acad Med 2004; 79: 244–49.

13. Hickson GB, Pichert, JW, Web LE, Gabbe SG. A complementary approach to promoting professionalism: Identifying, measuring, and addressing unprofessional behaviors. Acad Med 2007; 82: 1040–48.

Chapter 7

Pursuing Professionalism
(But not without an infrastructure)

Gerald B. Hickson, MD, and William O. Cooper, MD, MPH

You are a senior leader in an academic medical center. A junior surgical resident you have worked with has scheduled time to discuss some concerns:

> Dr. Resident states: "I feel miserable and guilty about my failure." Dr. Resident was asked to insert a central line on a patient. "We were a little slow getting everything assembled when Dr. Attending rushed in and asked, 'You're not finished yet? Which part of my instructions did you not understand?' I tried to explain. . . . Dr. Attending just proceeded to take over and insert the line. The problem is his prep was quick and he did not fully drape the patient. I just stood there. Now the patient is on pressors in the ICU and her blood culture is growing staph. I feel responsible. I just stood there. . . ."

As a medical leader within the health system, and as an individual with responsibilities for mentoring students and residents, how might you respond?

• Attempt to reassure Dr. Resident that a certain proportion of patients get central line associated bloodstream infections and that the failure to carefully prep is probably unrelated.

• Remind the resident of your physician wellness program, noting that all professionals have patients with bad outcomes. Suggest that it is important to understand these personal challenges early in a career and learn how to cope.

• Explain to the resident that sometimes when professionals are busy and stressed they can behave as described but that, "I know Dr. Attending and he is a really committed clinician. He was probably just having one of those days."

• Encourage the resident to share the concern with risk management and/or quality. "We have an event reporting system and you can always report and even do so anonymously."

• Contact Dr. Attending directly and share your concern about his unprofessional behavior.

These options represent just a few of many available. The decision about which action(s) to take in responding is complex and potentially influenced by the answers to several questions. Is the story true? Should you investigate to see if others observed the same event? But if the event is true as presented and you talk to Dr. Attending, how will he respond? He might thank you (but you doubt that will happen); he might even ask you who reported him and then seek to retaliate (i.e., verbally challenging Dr. Resident or negatively evaluating Dr. Resident's performance). Who else beyond Dr. Resident was impacted? What other health care professionals observed Dr. Attending's behavior? If leaders do not respond to verbal assaults or failures to follow evidence-based practices, how will it affect your culture of safety? Furthermore, isn't it the duty of every professional to do whatever is possible to prevent harm? On the other hand, if leaders spend all of their time policing individuals who on occasion fail to wash their hands or follow best practices in central line insertion, will there be enough time in the day to accomplish other important activities? Who wants to be a behavior monitor anyway?

How often do members of medical teams observe slips and lapses in professional performance and conduct? How do we help leaders understand how best to weigh the pros and cons of acting when they either observe or become aware of an event that seems inconsistent with the highest standards of the profession?

We assert that whereas much is written about professionalism and its noble tenets, far too little attention has been focused on understanding a critical component of professionalism—the commitment to group and self-regulation. We further assert that while it requires courage to examine one's own performance, it requires even more courage to assess and intervene on the behavior and/or performance of others. Furthermore, courage by itself is not sufficient, and leaders will fail to achieve the success they intend unless they are supported by the people, processes, and technology that provide an infrastructure designed to address single lapses in professionalism and facilitate early identification and intervention for those who appear to be associated with patterns of unprofessional behavior and/or performance.

What is professionalism and professional self-regulation?

As you reflect on how to respond to Dr. Resident, you pause and reflect on your personal goals for the practice of medicine and your view of what it means to be a professional, as well as your group's mission and goals for care delivery. Specifically, how does being a professional inform or influence your decisions and interactions with patients, families, learners, and colleagues?

Professionalism represents a commitment to cognitive and technical competence and to certain behavioral attributes that promote optimal team performance.[1] These behavioral attributes include a commitment to clear and effective communication, being available, modeling respect for others, and committing to reflect on how one's own behavior impacts the performance of others.

For example, professionals need to effectively communicate with peers and other colleagues about plans, instructions, and expectations to promote best outcomes. Availability may take the form of physical presence or response to communication, including answering pages for consults from colleagues or from nurses who are concerned about a change in a patient's status. Failing to respond threatens team function and on occasion directly affects patient outcomes. How often do nursing professionals hesitate to call and report a new finding because a clinician has a reputation for not responding or responding in a disrespectful way? We believe that real professionals model respect for others and value the dignity of all team members, including the patient and family. Finally, one of the most important distinguishing requirements of a professional is the commitment to be reflective. When a professional experiences an unintended outcome of care or is presented with a story or data suggesting his deviation from desired performance, he commits to reflect as appropriate and adjust his behaviors and performance accordingly.

Professional accountability and reliability

As you review your conversation with Dr. Resident, you conclude that public humiliation of a learner does not model respect and is not an effective means for communicating. That lapse should be addressed.

Failures to self- or group-regulate have a negative impact on all members of the health care team. Unprofessional behaviors, whether aggressive, passive-aggressive, or passive, threaten reliability and safety. Studies of teams in business settings suggest that negative behaviors modeled by one team member lead others to adopt negative mood and/or anger in interactions with others.[2,3] Unaddressed disruptive behaviors lessen trust among team members and can contribute to worse task performance as individuals are forced to monitor the disruptive professional's behavior and are not focused on their primary tasks. Distraction and lack of focus during medical practice contribute to slips and lapses.[4,5] Finally, as disruptive behaviors persist, team members may withdraw or leave the organization entirely.[6,7] Consider Dr. Attending's behavior with the central line insertion. Did his slip in professionalism "cause" the infection? It is never really possible to know, but his performance had an impact on Dr. Resident and perhaps on other team members in a variety of ways, including some team members who possibly may decide that it is acceptable to deviate from evidence-based practice.

Over the past decade, medical educators have focused attention on teaching many of the tenets of being professional.[8-10] We assert however that the collective dialogue has failed to include sufficient attention to the concept of self- and group-regulation and how to create effective plans to address clinicians who model unprofessional performance. It may be easier to sit in a lecture hall or classroom and discuss a vision of the noble professional than to consider practical issues such as how to address Dr. Attending's behavior. A leader might think, "Besides, if we keep focusing on this 'regulation' stuff, I might actually have to go and talk to Dr. Attending. He may not be so happy to hear from me, not refer patients to me, seek to retaliate, or choose to leave." Perhaps this is why professionals often talk about each other, but not to each other.[11]

A second incident

You (Dr. Leader) decide to speak with Dr. Attending, but before you can do so, a second event comes to your attention.

> A nurse reported in your organization's electronic event system: "Dr. Attending was examining a patient with an abscess. When he entered the room he did not foam in [wash his hands]. I offered a pair of gloves. He took the gloves from my hand, smiled, and dropped them in the trash, and said, 'No, thank you.' He then went back to examining the patient."

Professionals need an infrastructure

Established policy in Dr. Leader's hospital is for professionalism concerns to be entered into an electronic event reporting system. Such stories are reviewed by authorized personnel from the Department of Quality and Safety and then forwarded to a designated medical peer for face-to-face delivery. Creating a process to accomplish reliable delivery promoting accountability required years of work, dialogue, and consensus building. The plan was developed with a set of core principles in mind, including **justice**, **data certainty**, and a commitment to provide individual clinicians the **opportunity through feedback to develop personal insight**.[12] The overarching goal was **restoration**, giving the clinician who has strayed an opportunity to regain the honor of being a professional. **Justice** means that all professionals are subject to the same rules with respect to performance, data sharing, and accountability. Justice requires that there are no individuals with "special" value who for whatever reason are exempt because they have unique clinical skills or generate high levels of clinical revenue.[12]

Data certainty does not reflect the need for a p value <0.05, but refers to the notion that in the context of the individual's group or health system, as reports begin to accumulate, sharing seems reasonable and is done in a way that encourages personal insight.

Insight includes "both intellectual and emotional awareness of the nature, origin, and mechanisms of one's attitudes, feelings, and behavior,"[13] and is an essential prerequisite for individuals to take meaningful action toward change with a goal for a restoration of professional behavior and performance.

In reflecting about these guiding principles, we suggest that there are eight elements of an infrastructure required to support professionals to effectively and reliably handle the important challenge of self- and group-regulation.[1,14] They include:

1. Leadership commitment
2. Vision, mission, core values, and supportive policies
3. Surveillance/measurement tools to capture observations/data
4. Process for reviewing observations/data
5. Model to guide graduated interventions
6. Multi-level professional/leader training about professionalism and ways to equip clinicians to share data, promoting accountability
7. Resources to address the reasons that professionals fail to achieve intended outcomes, including ineffective or failing systems and human behavior
8. Resources to help other team members, patients, and families who may have suffered psychological or physical harm related to the behavior and performance of clinicians.

Of these eight elements, **leadership commitment** is key. By that we mean the willingness to:[1]

• Hold all team members accountable for modeling right behaviors and performance, whether related to washing hands, completing documentation, or treating other members of the medical team with respect.

• Enforce standards of practice and code of conduct consistently and equitably among all regardless of seniority or "special" value to the organization. (Special value may be defined based on an individual's unique skills and ability, record in amassing a large number of research grants or clinical revenue, playing a critical role in a unique clinical service, or personal or social relationships.) Real leaders will not "blink."

• Honor and recognize professionalism in action. Positive reinforcement of clinicians who exceed expectations helps to publically demonstrate the organization's commitment.

• Employ appropriate tools (i.e., reporting systems) designed to facilitate both early identification and reporting of slips and lapses in behavior and performance, and to give feedback in ways designed to promote insight and self-regulation.

• Provide resources to build and maintain the infrastructure to support professional self-regulation efforts. Sustaining a reliable approach to professional regulation is not possible if it is supported only by individuals' spare time.

Take a moment to reflect on the extent to which the system in which you work models leadership commitment to address "early and often" the behavior inconsistent with the concept of what it means to be a professional. In addition, think about your personal commitment to address behavior and performance issues among your colleagues. If you happened to walk into a unit and encountered Dr. Attending yelling at Dr. Resident, would you be willing and able to act? Promoting professionalism requires action.

Leaders also understand the need to create and disseminate **vision and mission statements** with associated **performance goals**. Creating a vision and mission is powerful. Consider the impact of the 100,000 Lives Campaign, as professionals across the United States committed to implement six evidence-based interventions to improve patient safety. It has been estimated that over 122,000 lives were saved as a result.[15] A medical group should also document its credo, a set of core values that define who its members are. For example, the Vanderbilt University Medical Center credo states: "I make those I serve my highest priority. I respect privacy and confidentiality. I communicate effectively. I conduct myself professionally. I have a sense of ownership. I am committed to my colleagues."[16] The elements of the credo are used to support performance evaluation, reinforcing a commitment to principles of professionalism. They also may be used to support dialogue between professional peers when an event occurs that appears to be inconsistent with the group's core values. Finally, new team members should be introduced to the group's vision, mission, goals, credo, and policies as a part of their onboarding. Such an approach facilitates early communication in those uncommon but unfortunately not rare circumstances when a new clinical colleague behaves in a way inconsistent with her letters of recommendation.

Group, health system, or hospital policies governing professional behavior and performance should be written in a way that align them with the credo and with a clearly articulated focus on safety. Medical groups should delineate codes of conduct that include definitions of acceptable and inappropriate behaviors. Policies should be developed that address a lack of tolerance for egregious behaviors or certain behaviors for which the law mandates a formal process for review,[17] including alleged violations of sexual boundaries, inappropriate physical touching, assertions of discrimination, or abuse. Finally, policies must outline clear protection for those who report "events," as the real or perceived threat of retaliation represents formidable barriers to safe reporting. Leaders of health care organizations must constantly be on guard for evidence of subtle and not so subtle ways that individuals seek to take retribution. Any confirmed "assault," verbal or otherwise, on a safety event reporter mandates an escalated response, including possible disciplinary actions.[1]

Necessary policies are effectively nullified when behaviors and performance inconsistent with the tenets of the profession and that undermine a culture of safety go unreported and unaddressed. Therefore an effective infrastructure includes **surveillance and measurement tools** with **defined processes for data review** and a tiered model for **feedback and accountability**. The development of surveillance and measurement tools and approaches for the review and sharing of data should include review by a broad range of professional leaders who must explicitly declare their support *before* specific individuals (i.e., performance outliers) are identified. Too often, new initiatives are launched and professionals with opportunities for performance improvement are identified, but leaders "blink" by publicly challenging the metrics after they are established or by rationalizing how in "this case" there exist special circumstances justifying the apparent poor performance. All of us are sometimes tempted to rationalize, but professional leaders establish and pursue the established plan regardless of who is identified—as long as the goal of the process is to bring insight and restoration. It is imperative that leadership become engaged early in the process and endorse each step of the data collection, assessment, delivery, and potential consequences for failure to respond.

All members of the team need to understand the critical aspects of a safety culture and accountability. Leaders should receive additional **training** on appropriate use of data and surveillance tools and how to promote accountability. For example, it is useful for a leader to develop skills in sharing observations of behavior that appear to undermine a culture of safety, both for individual reports and when there appears to be a pattern. Leaders should also be trained to identify various types of pushback and how to appropriately respond.

In addition, **resources for individuals** who fail to respond to interventions might include physical and/or mental health evaluations and help in addressing needs that might be identified. **Resources for staff** who may be impacted by negative behaviors should be made available, including critical incident debriefing or other resources through an employee assistance program.

Two important sources of data about professional performance deserve detailed description—the reported direct observations of patients and of medical team members, including other physicians, nurses, and allied health personnel. Patients routinely observe the behaviors and performance of health care team members; they and their families may experience such things as:

- Rude, disrespectful behavior—a patient who reported her physician said, "You don't need to ask questions. Just lay down here."
- Failure to communicate clearly—"Dr. X ended the visit abruptly and I had no idea what was supposed to happen next."
- Lack of access—"We had the test over a month ago and no one called us. Now we are told that there is a problem with the biopsy."

If organizations are committed, they convey to patients that their observations are valued and that the organization "wants to hear from them." Such an approach facilitates service recovery, the effort to systematically respond to any patient or family to address what they perceive is wrong.[18] Even though most individuals who observe unprofessional behavior will not speak up (perhaps only one out of forty to seventy dissatisfied patients),[19] a subset will, and analysis of their stories provides important data to support identification of professionals who model patterns of unprofessional conduct.[19–23]

Similarly, staff, including nurses, fellow physicians, and learners, observe their colleagues, and a subset will share their stories if they feel safe and trust the medical group to use their observations for improvement.[24] A nurse who reports through an event reporting system that a physician failed to respond to several pages and then suggested that the issue "was not her problem—call the cardiologist," seems to be identifying a problem with availability or taking responsibility. Another nurse who reports that a physician interrupted her phone call describing a change in patient status, asking her, "Are you stupid or are you illiterate? I wrote an order on this patient forty-five minutes ago," may be identifying an individual who has a problem with respect for others.

A graded response to stories, reports, and data

To support the pursuit of professional regulation, Dr. Leader's system adopted a professional accountability pyramid to direct the process and method of sharing.[1] The pyramid is built on the fact that the vast majority of professionals are seldom involved in any questions of behavior or performance. On the other hand, single events occasionally occur, like the resident's report about Dr. Attending's failure to follow best practices in line insertion. Staff observations are reviewed shortly after receipt by a member of the safety team. The purpose of the initial review is to identify any evidence of an event that requires a mandated evaluation (the black triangle in the lower right of the pyramid), including assertions of sexual boundary violations, physical assault, or assertions of discrimination or abuse.[1] Dr. Leader's system also has embraced mandated reviews with appropriate escalation and consequences for "egregious events" (the gray triangle in the lower right of the pyramid), such as seeking to retaliate

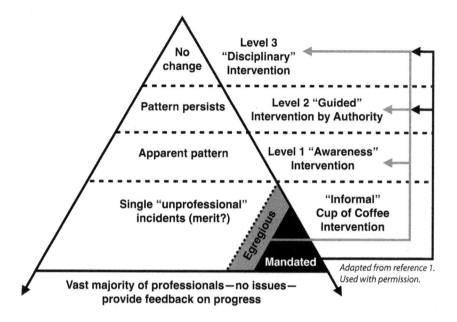

Adapted from reference 1.
Used with permission.

against someone who in good faith reports a safety concern. However, most reports (by patients or staff) do not call for mandated evaluation and should be shared with the named professional in an informal, non-judgmental, and respectful fashion (i.e., over a cup of coffee). For this reason, Dr. Leader's group has designated physician peer messengers by department, who are trained to deliver the individual reports.

When Dr. Attending and the "gloves in the trash" incident was reported, it was shared with the peer messenger. Dr. Peer called Dr. Attending and asked if they could get together briefly in Dr. Attending's office that day or the next. Once greetings concluded, Dr. Peer reminded Dr. Attending that staff members are encouraged to submit concerns about observed behaviors and performance that appear inconsistent with the group's credo. All such reports are reviewed and distributed for delivery. The process was established to support a culture of safety and it is assumed by the group that professionals want to know. At that point the essence of the story was shared and Dr. Peer respectfully paused, offering Dr. Attending an opportunity to respond. Dr. Attending paused briefly and then asserted, "I washed my hands before I entered the room. I always foam in and I don't know anything about throwing any gloves into a trash can." Dr. Peer responded, "I know you are committed to our focus on hand hygiene. As far as the part about gloves, it just didn't seem like you [no point in disputing], but I have to wonder about the details of the report. I just ask you to reflect back on the visit in question and I trust you to do whatever you think is right [no mandated policy or required action]. Dr.

Attending, you are a valued member of the team and that is why I am here to share with you and others whenever such reports are received."

The goal of a cup of coffee is to deliver a message about a single event and provide an opportunity for individual self-regulation and personal insight. Peer messengers are taught that cup of coffee conversations are not control contests or a chance to "fix" their colleagues. Such conversations are short (three to five minutes) and generally not documented, though the event precipitating the need for the conversation remains within the surveillance system for future reference as needed.

Of note, Dr. Leader's organization supports the timely delivery of professionalism reports without investigation if they do not represent egregious or mandated reporting events. Many if not most organizations and medical groups encourage the investigation of stories. In our view, this represents a process that increases conflict, seldom reveals the "truth," delays feedback, and is subject to the judgment of a few leaders who may either choose to the "look the other way" or in rare instances use the events to embarrass or humiliate. Because Dr. Leader's group has an effective surveillance system, he or she can afford to be patient. If the event is indeed isolated, there will not be additional reports entered into the surveillance system. However, if the event reflects just one occurrence of a pattern, there will most certainly be additional reports and opportunities for feedback to the named clinician.

The pyramid is constructed anticipating that some professionals will not respond to the cup of coffee, and those individuals will continue to accumulate complaints. Linking the pyramid to longitudinal data collection for both patient and staff complaints allows the group or system to establish thresholds to direct escalation as needed.[1]

Addressing potential patterns

It turns out that Dr. Attending has been mentioned in three previous staff reports. The dropped gloves incident is a fourth report. What does it mean to have three, four, or five reports in any defined time frame? A leader will not know without a surveillance system, data review, and an associated process to promote professional accountability.

Whenever clinicians are associated with a greater number of complaints than a threshold determined by the organization's leadership, the Chief Safety Officer prepares materials for review by the appropriate authority figure or authorized committee. Dr. Chair knows that eighty-five percent of group members have no complaints, ten percent have only one occasional complaint, and three percent (including Dr. Attending) have four or more complaints during a three-year audit period. In fact,

Dr. Attending is in the small group that accounts for over forty percent of all documented professionalism concern reports. As the leader, Dr. Chair decides to proceed with the awareness intervention as directed by the professionalism pyramid.

The goal of an awareness intervention, whether delivered by an authority figure or peer as a member of a professionalism committee, is to share with Dr. Attending that there appears to be a pattern of behavior or performance inconsistent with the organization's safety culture and to encourage self-reflection. The visit also provides notice that if the unprofessional behavior continues, the leader *may* have to escalate the intervention and become directive. The visit is preceded with a letter stamped confidential from Dr. Chair directed to Dr. Attending. The letter affirms the importance that the medical group places on professionalism and achieving the highest levels of patient safety and satisfaction. It reminds Dr. Attending of the system-wide agreement to share staff reports and reminds Dr. Attending that he has received several individual reports over the past several months, as well as the fact that complaints have continued to accumulate. He is reminded that the purpose of sharing is not to debate the merits of any specific report, but to encourage Dr. Attending to consider why in the aggregate his practice seems to be associated with more complaints than others. The letter serves as a request by Dr. Chair to set up a visit in *Dr. Attending's office* where the stories will be shared, as well as other data to encourage reflection.

At the time of the visit, Dr. Chair thanks Dr. Attending for making time and then proceeds to share the data suggesting that for some reason Dr. Attending's practice is associated with more staff complaints than others. To support the assertion, Dr. Attending is provided the individual complaint narratives, a table illustrating complaint type themes (e.g., communication, medical care, responsibility, professional integrity), a figure illustrating the distribution of all complaints about the physicians in the system with Dr. Attending labeled, and a copy of the group's professionalism policy. Dr. Chair provides several opportunities for Dr. Attending to respond and ask questions. As the visit concludes, Dr. Chair affirms that Dr. Attending is an important member of the team, but reminds Dr. Attending that the accumulation of staff reports does not seem consistent with the group's collective commitment to professionalism. He is asked to reflect on why it might be that his practice is associated with so many complaints. Dr. Attending is reminded that he will continue to receive follow-up about his complaint status on a regular basis and that most professionals who receive such peer-based feedback respond.[1,19] The leader is hopeful that Dr. Attending will respond as well. However "if complaints continue there *may* have to be an escalation in the level of intervention."

Training to conduct "awareness" interventions is case-based and leaders/peer messengers are taught how to address common pushbacks. In addition, training is designed to help leaders/peer messengers recognize and understand boundaries—awareness visits are not designed to be directive, to make a diagnosis, or suggest a treatment plan. A challenge faced by many leaders/messengers arises from a natural inclination to coach. Whereas most leaders are likely to be correct in their recommendations, providing direction at this point is not respectful and does not promote self-reflection and the self-regulation required in a safety culture. Offering advice also sets the leader/messenger up for an all-too-predictable pushback. Whenever a leader/messenger offers a suggestion and there is no subsequent evidence of performance improvement, when follow-up occurs, the recipient very often responds, "I did everything you suggested. This is all about *your* bad advice and one more example of *your* poor leadership."

Unfortunately, over the next few weeks Dr. Attending is named in two additional professionalism concerns.

> "I was shocked that Dr. Attending took a personal cell phone call right in the middle of the procedure. . . . It was scary and upsetting."
>
> The next week a scrub nurse reported that during a stressful point in a surgical procedure, Dr. Attending "grabbed the instrument out of my hand and told me to get the hell out of his operating room."

The group's professionalism policy directs that Dr. Chair and Dr. Leader are notified of the new reports and the need to consider a more directive intervention. In a guided intervention, leaders review the data and develop a plan designed to address whatever they think may be contributing to the problem, whether from a poorly functioning practice or system to physical or mental health challenges that may be affecting Dr. Attending's performance.[12] This level of professional help is possible only if collective leadership ensures adequate resources are available for evaluation and treatment. In our experience most individuals who reach the guided intervention level need to be directed for a mental and physical health screening evaluation. Prior to meeting with Dr. Attending, Dr. Chair develops a written plan that is reviewed and approved by an appropriate leader (dean, chief medical officer, or chief of staff), outlining the group's expectations, Dr. Attending's deficiencies (i.e., continued complaint generation), the mandated intervention (i.e., referral for a screening health evaluation), the potential consequence for failing to comply, the timeline for completion of the evaluation, and ongoing monitoring of performance. The guided intervention visit occurs in Dr. Chair's office.

While many individuals are able to, with appropriate assistance, address their unprofessional behaviors and reenter practice, a few will not. At this point, institutional commitment supported by unified leadership is critical, including policies that define unprofessional behavior, surveillance systems to permit reliable assessment and tracking of performance over time, a process and method for promoting accountability, and resources to provide colleagues an opportunity to improve. We assert such a process with predictable responses is fair, provides reasonable certainty that a peer needs assistance, provides an opportunity for individuals to develop personal insight, and allows change and restoration to the full honor of the profession. If individuals fail to respond, it is not fair to other members of the medical team that they continue to work, putting fellow professionals and patients at psychological or physical risk.[14,25-27]

Does any of this work?

Does any of this work? Is there really any hope of restoring Dr. Attending to the honor of the profession?

Support for a tiered approach to promote professional accountability is provided by a series of studies examining ways to change physician practice performance. Ray et al. demonstrated the effectiveness of academic detailing to improve physician prescribing practices, which resulted in sustained reductions in the contraindicated practice of prescribing chloramphenicol and tetracycline to young children.[28-30] An element of this program's success was data delivery by a professional peer and explanations that the colleague appeared to stand out from others. Building off the success of Ray and others, our research team considered whether the same methods (i.e., peer delivery of comparative data, delineation of expected professional norms supporting group accountability) would help to reduce malpractice risk for the small subset of physicians by discipline (two to eight percent) who are associated with a disproportionate share of malpractice claims and payments.[31,32] A series of studies showed that high claims experience physicians stand out because they consistently model behaviors described by their patients as unprofessional (e.g., being rude, failing to respond to questions, and communicating poorly).[21,22,31,33] High-risk physicians can be identified by coding and aggregating unsolicited patient complaint reports (a critical component of a professional surveillance system), yielding an index that is strongly associated with malpractice claims risk.[31] In a study in a large academic medical center, physicians at high risk (eight percent) were associated with more than forty percent of all group claims and greater than fifty percent of all dollars paid for defense, awards, and settlement costs.[31]

In considering the best approach to promote personal insight and practice change, we borrowed from the Ray model,[30] and created the Promoting Professionalism pyramid. Using an academic detailing model, unsolicited complaint reports were shared in person by trained peer messengers with clinicians identified as being at high risk. High-risk professionals were asked to reflect on why their practice was associated with so much dissatisfaction (compared with their peers) and therefore malpractice risk. Peer messengers encouraged professionals to consider changes in their practices that might reduce their risk, but were specifically trained not to coach the professionals. Since the first interventions, approximately 1,000 high-claims-risk physicians have been made aware that they appear to stand out. The vast majority of those who receive interventions respond with an eighty percent reduction in complaint risk score; a small number require the more directed or guided interventions.[34]

The same process and method for sharing data was successfully used in a health system-wide effort to improve hand hygiene rates.[35] Failure to follow hand hygiene best practice threatens safety and should be addressed in a fair and measured way. The infection prevention team created an aspirational goal, obtained leader and team member support, developed and implemented a surveillance tool, and used the process and model defined by the professional pyramid to promote accountability. Data and performance expectations were shared with individuals and unit leadership where improvement opportunities were identified. The coordinated effort resulted in improvements of hand hygiene from about sixty percent to greater than ninety percent throughout the health system, and an observed reduction in device-associated hospital-acquired infections.[35] Improving care requires a level of commitment to the principle of professional self-regulation supported by a robust infrastructure, which aligns with both the highest aspiration of the professional and society's goals for health care delivery.

What are the critical elements for success?

Creating an infrastructure as outlined in the following table is a requirement for any size clinical group interested in promoting professionalism and pursuing a safety culture. For Dr. Leader, the institution had clearly stated values and a fair, equitable, and balanced process for delivering interventions to Dr. Attending.

Such a system is built on trust. Individuals who report concerns either as patients or colleagues must trust that the institution is committed to reviewing and acting on information that suggests a "disturbance." They must also trust that if they speak up, even if they are mistaken in their observations, they will be safe from retribution. Efforts to retaliate against reporters must be dealt with swiftly, even if only suspected. Colleagues who appear to be accumulating too many stories must trust that data will be shared in a non-judgmental way, giving them an opportunity to respond. Leaders must trust that other leaders in the organization will not "blink" under any circumstances, when, for example, an individual who has received any level of intervention attempts to circumvent the chain of command and appeal to a more senior leader. Leaders must fairly and consistently hold all accountable. No one can have "special" status.

Infrastructure Elements for Promoting Process Reliability and Professional Accountability	
1. Leadership commitment	5. Model to guide graduated interventions
2. Mission, goals, core values, and supportive policies	6. Multi-level professional/leader training (on infrastructure and communication skills)
3. Surveillance tools to capture observations and reports	7. Resources to help address the causes of unnecessary variation in performance (both system and individual)
4. Processes for reviewing observations and reports	8. Resources to help those affected (psychological or physical harm)

Professional to professional

During the guided intervention, Dr. Attending was presented with a letter directing him to report for a screening evaluation through the institution's professional wellness program. The evaluation identified a number of stressors in Dr. Attending's life that he acknowledged were having an impact on his practice. Review of the surveillance data confirmed that the timing of Dr. Attending's complaints appeared to correspond with his life stressors. Supported by these observations, Dr. Attending's personal insight, the availability of professional mental health services, and a surveillance system to monitor Dr. Attending's ongoing performance, Dr. Chair decides that there is reason for optimism. If complaints continue to accumulate, however, Dr. Attending will face disciplinary action as directed in the medical group's bylaws. The hope is that a professional will respond and again become a role model.

Conclusion

Training in what it means to be a professional is a fundamental part of medical education for learners at all levels. The effectiveness of professionalism training is enhanced when conducted in a culture filled with positive role models. Such a culture is not possible without personal courage by leaders and professionals who understand the importance of self- and group-regulation. Efforts at self- and group-regulation can only be sustained if there is an established infrastructure to support identification and intervention when individuals fail to live up to the expected norms of the profession, including modeling respect for others and a commitment to follow evidence-based practices. Training in what it means to be professional must focus not solely on the noble tenets of professionalism, but also on how to build, utilize, and sustain a supporting infrastructure. In our opinion, to teach about the former in the absence of teaching about the latter is unprofessional.

References

1. Hickson GB, Pichert JW, Webb LE, Gabbe SG. A complementary approach to promoting professionalism: Identifying, measuring, and addressing unprofessional behaviors. Acad Med 2007; 82: 1040–48.

2. Felps WM, Mitchell TR, Byington E. How, when, and why bad apples spoil the barrel: Negative group members and dysfunctional groups. Research in Organizational Behavior—An Annual Series of Analytical Essays and Critical Reviews 2006; 27: 175–222.

3. Dimberg U, Öhman A. Behold the wrath: Psychophysiological responses to facial stimuli. Motiv Emotion 1996; 20: 149–82.

4. Lewicki RJ, Bunker, BB. Trust in Relationships: A Model of Trust and Development and Decline. In: Bunker BB, Rubin, JZ, editors. Conflict, Cooperation, and Justice: Essays Inspired by the Work of Morton Deutsch. San Francisco: Jossey-Bass; 1995.

5. Wageman R. The meaning of interdependence. In: Turner ME, editor. Groups at Work: Theory and Research. Hillsdale (NJ): Lawrence Erlbaum Associates; 2000: 197–218.

6. Schroeder DA, Steel JE, Woodell AJ, Bembenek AF. Justice within social dilemmas. Pers Soc Psychol Rev 2003; 7: 375–87.

7. Pearson CM, Porath, CL. On the nature, consequences and remedies of workplace incivility: No time for "nice"? Think again. Acad Management Exec 2005; 19: 7–18.

8. Mitchell P, Wynia M, Golden R, et al. Core Principles & Values of Effective Team-Based Health Care. Washington (DC): Institute of Medicine of the National Academies; 2012. https://www.nationalahec.org/pdfs/VSRT-Team-Based-Care-Principles-values.pdf.

9. Frankel AS, Leonard MW, Denham CR. Fair and just culture, team behavior, and leadership engagement: The tools to achieve high reliability. Health Serv Res 2006; 41 (4 Pt 2): 1690–1709.

10. Dupree E, Anderson R, McEvoy MD, Brodman M. Professionalism: A necessary ingredient in a culture of safety. Jt Comm J Qual Patient Saf 2011; 37:

447–55.

11. Moran SK, Sicher CM. Interprofessional jousting and medical tragedies: Strategies for enhancing professional relations. AANA J 1996; 64: 521–24.

12. Reiter CE III, Pichert JW, Hickson GB. Addressing behavior and performance issues that threaten quality and patient safety: What your attorneys want you to know. Prog Pediatr Cardiol 2012; 33: 37–45.

13. Mosby's Dictionary of Medicine, Nursing, & Health Professions. Ninth Edition. St. Louis (MO): Mosby; 2012.

14. Hickson GB, Moore IN, Pichert JW, Benegas M Jr. Balancing Systems and Individual Accountability in a Safety Culture. In: Berman S, editor. From the Front Office to the Front Line: Essential Issues for Health Care Leaders. Second Edition. Oakbrook Terrace (IL): Joint Commission Resources; 2011: 1–36.

15. Berwick DM, Calkins DR, McCannon CJ, Hackbarth AD. The 100,000 lives campaign: Setting a goal and a deadline for improving health care quality. JAMA. 2006; 295: 324–27.

16. Vanderbilt University Medical Center Credo; 2012. http://www.mc.vanderbilt.edu/root/vumc.php?site=Elevatesite&doc=19079.

17. Joint Commission on Accreditation of Health Care Organizations. Sentinel Event Alert 40: Behaviors that Undermine a Culture of Safety. Oakbrook Terrace (IL): Joint Commission on Accreditation of Health Care Organizations 2008 Jul 9; 40. http://www.jointcommission.org/assets/1/18/SEA_40.PDF.

18. Hayden AC, Pichert JW, Fawcett J, et al. Best practices for basic and advanced skills in health care service recovery: A case study of a re-admitted patient. Jt Comm J Qual Patient Saf 2010; 36: 310–18.

19. Pichert J, Hickson GB. Patients as Observers and Reporters in Support of Safety. In: Barach PR, editor. Pediatric and Congenital Cardiac Disease: Outcomes Analysis, Quality Improvement and Patient Safety. London: Springer-Verlag; in press 2014.

20. Carroll KN, Cooper WO, Blackford JU, Hickson GB. Characteristics of families that complain following pediatric emergency visits. Ambul Pediatr 2005; 5: 326–31.

21. Moore IN, Pichert JW, Hickson GB, et al. Rethinking peer review: Detecting and addressing medical malpractice claims risk. Vanderbilt Law Rev 2006; 59: 1175–1206.

22. Stelfox HT, Gandhi TK, Orav EJ, Gustafson ML. The relation of patient satisfaction with complaints against physicians and malpractice lawsuits. Am J Med 2005; 118: 1126–33.

23. Wiggleton C, Petrusa E, Loomis K, et al. Medical students' experiences of moral distress: Development of a web-based survey. Acad Med 2010; 85: 111–17.

24. Rosenstein AH, O'Daniel M. Disruptive behavior and clinical outcomes: Perceptions of nurses and physicians. Am J Nurs 2005; 105: 54–64; quiz 64–65.

25. Catchpole K, Mishra A, Handa A, McCulloch P. Teamwork and error in

the operating room: Analysis of skills and roles. Ann Surg 2008; 247: 699–706.

26. Mishra A, Catchpole K, Dale T, McCulloch P. The influence of non-technical performance on technical outcome in laparoscopic cholecystectomy. Surg Endosc 2008; 22: 68–73.

27. Shouhed D, Gewertz B, Wiegmann D, Catchpole K. Integrating human factors research and surgery: A review. Arch Surg 2012; 147: 1141–46.

28. Ray WA, Federspiel CF, Schaffner W. Prescribing of chloramphenicol in ambulatory practice. An epidemiologic study among Tennessee Medicaid recipients. Ann Intern Med 1976; 84: 266–70.

29. Ray WA, Federspiel CF, Schaffner W. Prescribing of tetracycline to children less than 8 years old. A two-year epidemiologic study among ambulatory Tennessee medicaid recipients. JAMA 1977; 237: 2069–74.

30. Schaffner W, Ray WA, Federspiel CF, Miller WO. Improving antibiotic prescribing in office practice. A controlled trial of three educational methods. JAMA 1983; 250: 1728–32.

31. Hickson GB, Federspiel CF, Pichert JW, et al. Patient complaints and malpractice risk. JAMA 2002; 287: 2951–57.

32. Hyman DA, Sage WM. Medical malpractice in the outpatient setting: Through a glass, darkly. JAMA Intern Med 2013; 173: 2069–70.

33. Mukherjee K, Pichert JW, Cornett MB, et al. All trauma surgeons are not created equal: Asymmetric distribution of malpractice claims risk. J Trauma 2010; 69: 549–54.

34. Pichert JW, Moore IN, Karrass J, et al. An intervention model that promotes accountability: Peer messengers and patient/family complaints. Jt Comm J Qual Patient Saf 2013; 39: 435–46.

35. Talbot TR, Johnson JG, Fergus C, et al. Sustained improvement in hand hygiene adherence: Utilizing shared accountability and financial incentives. Infect Control Hosp Epidemiol 2013; 34: 1129–36.

Remediation

Chapter 8
Clinical Skills Remediation: Strategy for Intervention of Professionalism Lapses
Anna Chang, MD

his chapter brings the literature and practice of clinical skills guidance and remediation in medical education to the discussion of best practices in medical professionalism. First, it describes differences, and then similarities, between the approaches to low performance in clinical skills and professionalism. Next, it examines the applicability of a five-step clinical skills remediation and guidance strategy to address professionalism lapses. Finally, it suggests individual and systems approaches to the remediation of learners and colleagues who need guidance in medical professionalism.

Case example from clinical skills

Dear Student,

We regret to inform you that you have failed your clinical skills examination in the areas of history-taking, physical examination, clinical reasoning, and patient communication skills. Your performance is in the lowest 2% of the class and your score does not meet the minimum threshold for passing. You are now required to meet with the course director for remediation . . .

Letters like this notify some medical students each year of unexpected failing performance on clinical skills examinations. At one medical school, this notice at the end of a foundational clinical skills course informs a handful of second-year students about performance that is below expected competence on a multi-station standardized patient objective structured clinical examination (OSCE) final examination. Since the 1990s, most U.S. medical schools have required student participation in standardized patient clinical skills examinations, with a median annual cost of $50,000 per examination in 2005.[1] For most medical students, examinations like this are among the first in a series of high-stakes clinical skills examinations to ensure that they achieve minimum expected competence in the clinical skills required to advance to medical school graduation, residency entry, and board certification.[1]

Studies have reported strategies to guide the steps following a student's failure to progress to the next stage of training because of below-expected competence performance compared with milestones in the competency domain of patient care.[2] In recent years, scholarship in this area has examined various aspects of guidance and remediation in medical education, from tools for early identification of struggling learners, to the effect of performance data on learning goals, to systematic reviews of remediation processes among U.S. medical schools.[3–6] Thus, the field of clinical skills guidance and remediation is on the path of building an evidence base of best practices to guide educators and institutions.

Clinical skills versus professionalism: Differences

Many educators would likely point out some important differences between the approach to assessment and remediation of clinical skills and the approach applied to lapses in medical professionalism.

First, structured checklists along with global rating scales are now routinely used in assessment and standard-setting of formative and summative clinical skills examinations.[1,7] Faculty members or standardized patients complete checklists after simulated clinical encounters.[7,8] Passing performance can be determined by criterion-referenced or normative standard setting methods.[1,8] In other examinations, checklists of key history or physical examination items are applied to the written post-encounter clinical note to assess the learners' clinical reasoning.[8] These real or standardized patient examinations with the use of checklists occur multiple times throughout medical school, and students are no longer allowed to advance to licensure without demonstrating clinical skills competence.[9] Similar assessment systems may be less consistently applied to the competency domain of professionalism.

Second, identification and remediation of deficits in the technical aspects of clinical skills may be perceived as less emotional, and therefore easier, for both faculty and learners than lapses in professionalism. Faculty members find it challenging to fail learners.[10] "Millennial generation" learners thrive with positive feedback.[11] One study shows that students are more likely to give constructive feedback about technical deficits (e.g., physical examination technique) when randomly grouped with peers.[12] Only after longitudinal peer cohorts have spent years together do students begin to develop the trust and comfort that allows them to give constructive feedback about more personal and interpersonal learning needs (e.g., communication skills).[12] Thus, it is possible that low performers in general clinical skills may be identified with more ease than those who demonstrate professionalism lapses.

Third, most schools have additional guidance programs for clinical skills deficits, as well as processes to measure improvement after remediation.[2,6] Structured remediation programs for the more technical skills of medicine, such as key history items or physical examination technique, are common in medical schools today.[2,6,13] On the other hand, similar pre-existing systems to support learners with professionalism lapses are rarely reported in the literature, may not be as prevalent in practice, and may develop on an *ad hoc* basis in response to individual issues.[14] Faculty members hesitate to point out learner performance deficits for multiple reasons, particularly if they are uncertain about the availability of remediation options.[10] The lack of remediation programs in professionalism may affect the identification of those with professionalism lapses. Furthermore, most medical schools repeat the clinical skills examination after remediation programs, and almost all schools report having a process to reassess clinical skills competence.[6] Thus, one approach to begin to close the gap of differences is to develop similarly robust identification, remediation, and reassessment processes for learners and colleagues in the domain of medical professionalism.

Clinical skills and professionalism: Similarities

There are also notable similarities between the principles and steps in working with those with additional learning needs in clinical skills and in medical professionalism.

First, learners demonstrate their abilities in clinical skills or professionalism, as well as in other competency domains, in overlapping and integrated ways while participating in many of the same activities in the classroom environment and in the clinical setting.[15] The movement towards the use of entrustable professional activities as an educational assessment framework advocates for the unit of measurement of physician skills to be an integrated activity, rather than deconstructed competencies.[16] Viewed through this lens, skills in history taking, physical examination, communication, and professionalism are interrelated elements of a single connected whole.

Second, the strategy for remediation in any competency domain begins with identification of those who are performing poorly compared to performance standards using objective measurement tools.[2] The low performer then receives performance data and feedback, as well as guidance to develop effective learning plans that target the deficit.[6] The plan is put into action for a period of time, and the learner is then retested by objective measures to determine the outcome of remediation.[2] With these steps, the approach to low-performing learners in both clinical skills and professionalism can be remarkably similar.

Finally, competence in general clinical skills and competence in medical professionalism are intertwined and essential to the physician's role on the clinical team, and the physician's duty to patients.[17,18] For example, communication skills as applied to gathering and sharing information are among the most important clinical skills in the patient encounter, and are simultaneously crucial for aspects of professionalism that involve interactions with the patient. As such, the outcomes of remediation for both have meaning for individual patient care as well as health care systems. Thus, the reasons for, and end result of, remediation for both general clinical skills and medical professionalism have significant impact on outcomes such as patient safety, patient satisfaction, and quality of care.

Why remediate?

> But if I accept you as you are, I will make you worse; however if I treat you as though you are what you are capable of becoming, I help you become that.
>
> —Goethe

Despite individual and systems challenges inherent to each step of the process—from identification of low performers, to accurately describing the deficit, to designing a remediation program, to measuring outcomes—there are important reasons to pursue this path for learners in need. Medical educators hold a dual responsibility to their learners and to their learners' future patients. To fulfill the responsibility to their learners, educators must begin with the belief that each person has the ability to improve his or her performance and has the right to receive feedback and guidance that contribute to continued development as a professional. To fulfill the responsibility to their learners' future patients, educators need to assess learner performance with objectivity, apply skillful communication with courage to describe any deficits, and commit to participate in remediation whenever appropriate.

The following section describes a step-wise strategy for remediation drawn from lessons learned from clinical skills that can be adapted and applied to work in medical professionalism.

A sample remediation strategy in five steps:
Closing the gap between performance and expectations

This five-step strategy, beginning with identification of the deficit and ending with measurement of outcomes after remediation, can be used to frame the approach to helping learners with lapses in medical professionalism.

Step 1: Early Identification

The first step calls for early identification of learner deficits—a challenge for educators. As noted earlier, faculty can be reluctant to point out trainee problems for a number of reasons, including lack of documentation, lack of knowledge of what to document, the anticipation of a negative experience with an appeals process, and lack of remediation options.[10] Furthermore, medical educators are invested in the success of their learners, and cognitive psychologists have demonstrated that commitment to a process (e.g., teaching) can result in a higher likelihood of believing in positive results (i.e., learner competence) even if evidence exists to the contrary.[19] This belief may tempt educators to search for, or accept, situational reasons for poor performance from their learners. But to consistently achieve optimal learner performance, it is important to keenly differentiate between one-time contextual events and patterns of repeated low performance that point to a need for additional guidance.

The importance of early identification is confirmed by studies demonstrating that performance deficits, if not identified and addressed, tend to persist. Klamen et al. described a statistically robust correlation between low performance in clinical skills examinations in year two and in year four (OR 20, p=0).[4] Chang et al. reported that communication and professionalism deficits reported in core clerkship ratings (OR 1.79, p=0.008) and student progress review meetings (OR 2.64, p=0.002) predict failure in year four clinical skills examinations.[3] Studies show that early identification allows learners who need additional guidance the time and opportunity to develop and enact targeted learning plans to improve performance.[20]

When confronted with data of low performance after high-stakes assessments in the later years of school, students often ask: "Why didn't you tell me this earlier?" Studies confirm that educators do have data to identify learners with a pattern of professionalism lapses, and that sustained difficulties tend to track over time.[3,21] While educators may wish to believe that silence is kinder or allows learners more time to improve on their own, this erroneous assumption can actually hurt both learners and their future patients. Thus, early identification is an important first step.

Step 2: Objective data

This step identifies the gap by using objective measures or measurements to compare the learner's performance with expected milestones. For medical knowledge and clinical skills, a number of assessment tools are routinely used, including written examinations, oral examinations, simulated and real patient OSCEs, global ratings, direct observation, portfolio, 360° evaluation, etc.[22] Fifty-five tools were identified just for direct observation of clinical skills with real patients.[23] Approximately eighty to ninety percent of U.S. medical schools conduct simulated clinical skills examinations in years two, three, or four.[1] The majority (80%) use standardized patient checklists, and some (21%) use faculty checklists or global assessment scales to score clinical encounters.[2] Most (60%) use normative grading strategies, with the rest using criterion-referenced (21%) or a combination (18%).[2]

While there are flaws and challenges with any single assessment tool, there are important reasons to apply a combination of assessment tools to determine performance in every competency domain.[22] First, multiple groups of assessors (e.g., teachers, peers, standardized patients, real patients, clinical staff) can identify in learners similar deficits using different assessment tools at different times.[3] Second, even assessment tools designed primarily for measuring performance in one domain (e.g., clinical reasoning in a clinical skills examination) can identify lapses in performance in other domains (e.g., fabrication of clinical findings pointing to lapses in knowledge and professionalism).[15,24] To move successfully to the next step in this remediation strategy, it is important that the educator and the learner use the same data to establish agreement about the gap between performance and expectations.

Step 3: Shared understanding

After objective data establishes a gap between performance and expectations, the learner and the educator begin the process of building a shared understanding. Educators begin with the knowledge that learners need data and guidance—not just data alone—to identify their deficits and learning plans.[25] This guidance begins with a one-on-one meeting between the student and the educator in which a conversation about performance is built on a foundation of rapport, trust, and support.[13] Important techniques include listening, summarizing, responding to emotions, expressing support, and redirecting towards the learning objective. Some sample words to use include:

- "We are meeting today to discuss your performance in . . ."
- "What is your interpretation of . . ."
- "Here are some additional perspectives on . . ."
- "May we agree to work on improving . . ."

Some educators assume that learners will be able to correctly identify their learning needs and develop corrective plans on their own if given numerical and narrative evidence of low performance and even comparative cohort data. But in one study, only half of all students who failed a high-stakes clinical skills examination in the area of communication skills were able to develop learning goals in that area without faculty guidance, even after receiving individual and comparative examination results indicating failing performance, in both qualitative and quantitative formats.[25] This has potential implications for remediation in professionalism lapses. The debate to reach agreement on a shared definition of low performance in communication skills and professionalism skills can become mired in gray areas considered to be subjective, personal, emotional, and challenging. With low performing learners, educators cannot simply deliver performance data and leave learners alone to determine accurate next steps for improvement without guidance.[26,27]

Step 4: Learning plans

The strategy continues with a focus on two aspects of the learning plan: writing effective learning plans, and putting them into action.

After the educator and the learner have established a shared understanding of the learning gap as well as explored the need to develop targeted learning plans, the learner should be encouraged to initiate the process of drafting learning plans.[25] This step is important in reinforcing learner ownership and commitment, as well as demonstrating to educators where learners are starting from in their understanding and synthesis of the information thus far. One common acronym is SMART, indicating that effective learning plans are specific, measurable, attainable, relevant, and time-bound.[28] A sample ineffective learning plan might be: "I will read more" or "I will not be late." More effective learning plans are specific (e.g., "I will practice X skill"), measurable (e.g., "with the next three patients to achieve Y performance level"), and time-bound (e.g., "over the next two weeks). One study demonstrated that ninety-six percent of fourth-year students write specific learning goals with minimal written instructions.[25] However, without guidance, learners may not choose to write learning plans that address the most important areas of deficit, or may not know how to develop an effective plan to address target deficits.[25]

Putting learning plans into action may include sequential or multipronged approaches of deliberate practice in different formats and settings. Strategies include meetings between the faculty and the learner for role play and practice, additional or elective clinical experiences in environments that allow skills building, standardized patient cases in simulated clinical skills environments, peer learning, small groups observation and feedback, and others.[2,6,27,29–31]

Many U.S. medical schools employ group learning activities for deliberate practice in the context of remediation.[6] Peer learners, even those who have additional learning needs themselves, are effective teachers and feel safe in small group settings in the context of remediation.[29] While educators' confidence in their own ability to help learners remediate is generally low and is lowest for professionalism (2.96 on a scale of 1 = strongly disagree to 5 = strongly agree), their confidence increases with group practice options for learners.[6] In other words, when faculty are able to access group learning activities as a tool for remediation, they feel more confident participating in remediation for learners with lapses in professionalism.

Learners also may perceive feedback from peers as being more authentic, less threatening, and more understandable. Observation shows that learners have different strengths and weaknesses, and often complement each other when learning in small groups. Perhaps simply sharing the task of remediation in the form of group activities builds a learning community and decreases the resistance and activation energy needed for identification and remediation.[27]

Step 5: Measuring outcomes

The final step of this strategy is the measurement of outcomes after remediation. This remains a challenging task in every competency domain. The precise definition of developmentally appropriate performance goals, assessment tools, and standard setting strategies can seem to be elusive moving targets.

Approximately seventy-five percent of schools report retesting after clinical skills remediation with the same or different standardized patient examination cases.[6] However, many repeat examinations are less complex or more targeted in an effort to assess for minimum competence. The complexities of different standard-setting strategies likely also affect individual outcomes. With normative standard setting, educators find it challenging to choose the most appropriate cohort for comparison. Since the examination itself is often different from the original, educators are challenged with applying criterion-based scoring strategies to a retest applicable to only a few learners because it can require an intensive time investment from a group of experts to define appropriate cutoff scores.[8] And finally, with different competency-based education frameworks, educators debate the use of combinations of frameworks consisting of developmentally progressive milestones, non-overlapping competencies, or integrated entrustable professional activities, or others.[32] Thus, while somewhat cleaner measurement tools exist for clinical skills performance, more science is needed in both clinical skills and professionalism in assessment of remediation outcomes.

Summary: The science, the art, and the unknown of remediation
The science of remediation

The literature of remediation in medical education has been active since 2000, yet the science is still young. In the area of clinical skills remediation, scholarship has included surveys of medical school remediation processes, systematic reviews of remediation programs, books with expert recommendations, studies showing early identification predictors of struggling learners, and limited outcomes of remediation. In terms of timeline, the domain of clinical skills may be somewhat ahead of that on medical professionalism in building a robust body of work on assessment tools and remediation strategies. However, the progress made in defining medical professionalism lays the groundwork for next steps in practice and research, which may include development and validation of assessment tools, studies of remediation strategies, and descriptions of learner and systems outcomes.

The art of remediation

Success factors in the practice of remediation are rooted in the human experience of learning and achievement. Early identification of struggling learners is critical to allow for early intervention, which is often fruitful. The educator and learner begin with a one-on-one meeting to establish trust, safety, and shared goals. They then agree on performance data, performance expectations, and learning plans. One recommendation worth considering is framing the process as guidance for continuous improvement of performance rather than as remediation for failing performance. Educators could describe an invitation-only guidance program aimed at increasing the learner's future performance. This simple reframing can help learners to begin with an open mind for learning rather than dwelling on blame or shame. A second recommendation is to challenge the learner to actively initiate and own the process of learning. One example is having learners write and revise their own learning plans with faculty guidance along the way. Sometimes educators can be so eager to teach that they take over learner tasks in active learning. Expectations of active learning prevent the occasional surprising discovery of how little might be retained by the passive learner at the end of intense teaching.

The unknown of remediation: Shared challenges between remediation of clinical skills and professionalism lapses

Finally, there are remarkable parallels between the domains of clinical skills and medical professionalism in what remains to be learned in remediating learners or clinicians whose performance is below expected competence. These questions remain:

- What *is* the deficit?
- Do we aim to change the learner's attitude, or is changing behavior sufficient?
- What are effective strategies to guide learning in remediation?
- How do educators reserve time for remediation in the core curriculum?
- How do we systematically document performance after deliberate practice?

- What data contribute to reassessment other than absence of negative reports?
- What if improvement is not consistent across settings or over time?
- What is the end point of remediation?
  - For example, is it when the learner demonstrates adequate performance once, or more than once? In one context, or in more than one?
  - Is it when educators have built such a robust scaffold around these learners to get them barely over the threshold of competence that it cannot be sustained in a busy health care system to maintain adequate performance?
  - Or is remediation over when we find out that the behavior cannot be changed?

The future of remediation in the field of medicine should include studies of effectiveness of remediation strategies, data on long-term learner and patient outcomes after remediation, and the development of comprehensive systems approaches to professional development that cross silos of competency domains or course structures. In addition, participating in remediation may be an opportunity for learners to gain insight into generalizable ways to improve performance. Ultimately, effective learning programs initially developed for remediation could be expanded to improve everyone's performance with individual learning plans in all competency domains, and not just those who have already demonstrated lapse or failure. In this way, remediation programs would become one part of a whole system of competency-based learning and assessment in the continuum of lifelong learning, from undergraduate medical education, to graduate medical education, to clinical practice.

Conclusions

Effective practices of guidance and remediation for clinical skills and medical professionalism are important to medical education and clinical medicine. Lessons learned and practical strategies from clinical skills remediation can be adapted and applied to guidance of those with professionalism lapses. Systematic approaches to remediation in the domain of medical professionalism would move the field forward in fulfilling our duty to our colleagues and our patients.

Acknowledgments

Dr. Chang's work on clinical skills remediation was supported by the University of California San Francisco (UCSF) School of Medicine, the UCSF Haile T. Debas Academy of Medical Educators Innovations Funding Program, and the UCSF Medical Education Research Fellowship. Her work in clinical skills assessment is informed by participation as a member school faculty in the California Consortium for the Assessment of Clinical Competence, and as faculty on the Test Materials Development Committee for the National Board of Medical Examiner's USMLE Step 2 Clinical Skills Examinations.

References

1. Hauer KE, Hodgson CS, Kerr KM, et al. A national study of medical student clinical skills assessment. Acad Med 2005; 80 (10 Suppl): S25–29.

2. Hauer KE, Teherani A, Irby DM, et al. Approaches to medical student remediation after a comprehensive clinical skills examination. Med Educ 2008; 42: 104–12.

3. Chang A, Boscardin C, Chou CL, et al. Predicting failing performance on a standardized patient clinical performance examination: The importance of communication and professionalism skills deficits. Acad Med 2009; 84 (10 Suppl): S101–104

4. Klamen DL, Borgia PT. Can students' scores on preclerkship clinical performance examinations predict that they will fail a senior clinical performance examination? Acad Med 2011; 86: 516–20.

5. Chang A, Chou CL, Teherani A, Hauer KE. Clinical skills-related learning goals of senior medical students after performance feedback. Med Educ 2011; 45: 878–85.

6. Saxena V, O'Sullivan PS, Teherani A, et al. Remediation techniques for student performance problems after a comprehensive clinical skills assessment. Acad Med 2009; 84: 669–76.

7. Epstein RM, Hundert EM. Defining and assessing professional competence. JAMA 2002; 287: 226–35.

8. Wass V, Van der Vleuten C, Shatzer J, Jones R. Assessment of clinical competence. Lancet 2001; 357: 945–49.

9. Papadakis MA. The Step 2 clinical-skills examination. N Engl J Med 2004; 350: 1703–05.

10. Dudek NL, Marks MB, Regehr G. Failure to fail: The perspectives of clinical supervisors. Acad Med 2005; 80 (10 Suppl): S84–87.

11. Bing-You RG, Trowbridge RL. Why medical educators may be failing at feedback. JAMA 2009; 302: 1330–31.

12. Chou CL, Masters DE, Chang A, et al. Effects of longitudinal small-group learning on delivery and receipt of communication skills feedback. Med Educ 2013; 47: 1073–79.

13. Chang A, Chou CL, Hauer KE. Clinical skills remedial training for medical students. Med Educ 2008; 42: 1118–19.

14. Hauer KE, Ciccone A, Henzel TR, et al. Remediation of the deficiencies of physicians across the continuum from medical school to practice: A thematic review of the literature. Acad Med 2009; 84: 1822–32.

15. Teherani A, O'Sullivan P, Lovett M, Hauer KE. Categorization of unprofessional behaviours identified during administration of and remediation after a comprehensive clinical performance examination using a validated professionalism framework. Med Teach 2009; 31: 1007–12.

16. ten Cate O. Entrustability of professional activities and competency-based training. Med Educ 2005; 39: 1176–77.

17. Irvine D. The performance of doctors. I: Professionalism and self regulation in a changing world. BMJ 1997; 314: 1540–42.

18. Irvine D. The performance of doctors. II: Maintaining good practice, protecting patients from poor performance. BMJ 1997; 314: 1613–15.

19. Kahneman D. Thinking, Fast and Slow. New York: Farrar, Straus and Giroux; 2010.

20. Klamen DL, Williams RG. The efficacy of a targeted remediation process for students who fail standardized patient examinations. Teach Learn Med 2011; 23: 3–11.

21. Papadakis MA, Teherani A, Banach MA, et al. Disciplinary action by medical boards and prior behavior in medical school. N Engl J Med 2005; 353: 2673–82.

22. Epstein RM. Assessment in Medical Education. N Engl J Med 2007; 356: 387–96.

23. Kogan, JR., Holmboe ES, Hauer KE. Tools for direct observation and assessment of clinical skills of medical trainees: A systematic review. JAMA 2009; 302: 1316–26.

24. Friedman MH, Connell KJ, Olthoff AJ, et al. Medical student errors in making a diagnosis. Acad Med 1998; 73 (10 Suupl): S19–21.

25. Chang A, Chou CL, Teherani A, Hauer KE. Clinical skills-related learning goals of senior medical students after performance feedback. Med Educ 2011; 45: 878–85.

26. Durning SJ, Cleary TJ, Sandars J, et al. Perspective: Viewing "strugglers" through a different lens: How a self-regulated learning perspective can help medical educators with assessment and remediation. Acad Med 2011; 86: 488–95.

27. Steinert Y. The "problem" learner: Whose problem is it? AMEE Guide No. 76. Med Teach 2013; 35: e1035–45.

28. Hamilton M. Putting words in their mouths: The alignment of identities with system goals through the use of Individual Learning Plans. Brit Educ Res J 2009; 35: 221–42.

29. Chou CL, Chang A, Hauer KE. Remediation workshop for medical students in patient-doctor interaction skills. Med Educ 2008; 42: 537.

30. Cleland J, Leggett H, Sandars J, et al. The remediation challenge: Theoretical and methodological insights from a systematic review. Med Educ 2013; 47: 242–51.

31. Kalet A, Chou CL. Remediation in Medical Education: A Mid-Course

Correction. New York: Springer; 2013.

32. Pangaro L, ten Cate O. Frameworks for learner assessment in medicine: AMEE Guide No. 78. Med Teach 2013; 35: e1197–210.

Chapter 9

Remediating Professional Lapses of Medical Students: Each School an Island?

Richard M. Frankel, PhD

Remediation: (Latin) *Mederi* = to heal + *re* = again.
Definition: to put right or reform[1]

I recently attended the Association of American Medical Colleges (AAMC) 2014 Midwest Regional Group on Educational Affairs Meeting in Cleveland, Ohio, where my colleagues and I conducted a workshop on remediating professionalism lapses among medical students. At the beginning of my portion of the workshop, which was devoted to describing the professionalism remediation program at Indiana University School of Medicine, I asked the audience of sixty or so participants, "How many of you approach your remediation meetings with students with optimism, energy, and enthusiasm?" Not a single hand was raised. I then asked, "How many of you have received any formal training in how to conduct remediation meetings with students or are aware of any national guidelines or best practices in this area?" Again, no hands were raised. Finally, I asked, "How many of you have on your bucket list of things you want to accomplish in your medical education careers remediating medical student professionalism lapses? Amidst smiles and laughter, no one responded by raising a hand.

After having served as the professionalism competency director at a large medical school for nine years, and as a medical educator with three decades of experience, I was not surprised by these responses. In fact, they confirmed or reconfirmed elements of my own experience, namely, that remediation of professional lapses among medical students can be challenging; that each faculty member responsible for professionalism remediation works in isolation, and that there are few specific resources available for how to effectively conduct remediation encounters with students. The one area that felt at odds with my own experience was the bucket list question. Although it was not on my list initially, I have found my remediation encounters with students to be immensely rewarding and meaningful.

My goals in this chapter are threefold: first, I describe the professionalism competency program at Indiana University School of Medicine and the steps involved in the remediation process; next, I present three cases to illustrate my approach to the remediation encounter and its similarities to interviewing difficult patients; finally, I offer analysis, commentary, and suggestions for some steps that might be taken to stimulate national dialog around remediation processes and outcomes.

In the beginning . . .

In October of 2004, I became the third professionalism Competency Director (CD) at Indiana University School of Medicine, a position that was created in 1999 when the school adopted what was then only the second comprehensive undergraduate medical school competency curriculum in the United States. The curriculum was adopted after seven years of self-study and covered nine core competencies, including:

1. Effective communication
2. Basic clinical skills
3. Using science to guide diagnosis, management therapeutics, and prevention
4. Life-long learning
5. Self-awareness, self-care, and personal growth
6. The social and community contexts of health care
7. Moral reasoning and ethical judgment
8. Problem solving
9. Professionalism and role recognition.

The overall competency curriculum has been fully implemented since 1999. Each competency has a statewide director, a portion of whose salary is paid by the Dean's Office.

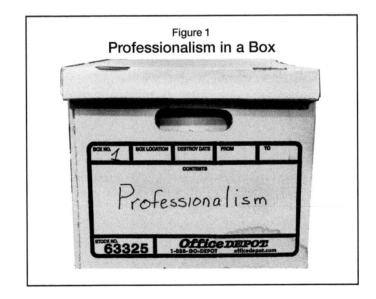

Figure 1
Professionalism in a Box

In my first week as CD, a box (see Figure 1) with articles, books, pamphlets, and videotapes was delivered to my office from the previous director, who had retired and moved to another state. The accompanying note congratulated me, wished me well, and said that the box contained all the material on professionalism that he had collected during his tenure. I was, of course, happy to get the material and immediately began digging into its contents. Many of the papers defining professionalism were familiar to me from work and teaching I had already done in the area. So, too, were the debates about whether professionalism consists of a set of timeless precepts and values or whether it is more like a complex adaptive system, a complex contextual cultural construct that changes as societal attitudes and values change.[2–7] As important and complex as this debate was, what struck me as interesting, and somewhat concerning considering the fact that I was going to have to do real-time remediation meetings with medical students, was the scarcity of material on how to actually conduct such meetings. As I reviewed the published literature I became alarmed about the paucity of research and outcome studies that have looked at best practices for remediating clinical skills in general,[8] and professionalism lapses of undergraduate medical students, in particular.[9,10] What there was tended to be based on small samples from individual schools with little practical guidance on what to look for, how to act, and how to assess success or failure of remediation efforts, especially given the gravity of decisions being made about students' career aspirations in medicine.

For example, Buchanan et al. suggest the following steps be taken in the remediation encounter: (1) confirm the lapse, (2) understand the context, (3) communicate and discuss in a mutually respectful manner, (4) encourage self-reflection, (5) agree on a plan for remediation, (6) document the interventions, and (7) construct a plan for follow-up.[11] While checklists of this sort are undoubtedly helpful, they are insensitive to the face-to-face interactional contexts in which remediation meetings take place. I needed practical strategies for how to approach my meetings with students, and guidance on what to say and do, not a checklist of topics to cover.

Mechanics of the professionalism competency at IUSM

In addition to an academic transcript, each student at IUSM carries a competency transcript that appears on a combined grade sheet. Failure to satisfactorily pass the competency curriculum means that a student is not qualified to graduate from the medical school. Students must demonstrate competency at three different levels.

To qualify for **Level 1** status, students must be able to:

1. Describe to others the core behavioral abilities of the IUSM competency in professionalism—excellence in humanism, accountability, and altruism.

2. Understand the acquisition of professional abilities as *phronesis* (practical wisdom).

3. Identify professional behaviors ranging from expected (normative) to exemplary, to unprofessional in both the formal and informal curriculum.

By the time of graduation all students must have achieved **Level 2** status and have:

1. Mastered core professionalism skills in teams.

2. Be able to articulate expected professional behaviors under stressful or challenging circumstances.

3. Demonstrate the core abilities of professionalism in all IUSM-related interactions with colleagues, faculty, staff, administrators, patients, the health care team, and others.

Level 3 requires students to select three of the nine competencies to learn about in greater depth than the standard curriculum. To obtain **Level 3** in Professionalism, students select a topic that will affect their learning in future stages of their careers, for example, in residency or practice. Working with a faculty mentor, students seeking Level 3 do research or observe in one or more actual settings, keeping a log of what they encounter. The log is then used as data for analyzing formal and informal elements of professionalism in the chosen setting(s). Students submit a

Figure 2
Competency Management Pathway

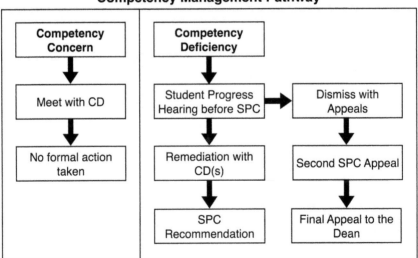

final report describing their findings and what they have learned about professionalism that will affect them as they progress in their career.

Managing the professionalism competency: The Director's role

The CD's role consists of three main functions:

1. Developing and maintaining the professionalism curriculum for medical students across all four years of training.

2. Acting as a resource for students and faculty with concerns about their own or others' professional behavior.

3. Serving as the "remediation arm" of the Student Promotions Committee (SPC) where cases of unprofessional behavior are adjudicated.

In this chapter I will deal primarily with the third function of remediating professionalism concerns and lapses.

Figure 2 illustrates the competency management pathway. A course director, clerkship director, or faculty member from any of the nine school of medicine campuses begins the process by entering a competency concern or an isolated deficiency (ID) in the statewide electronic evaluation system. Competency concerns generally fall into the category of minor professionalism issues such as appropriate dress for class or clinic, or major lapses such as cheating or failure to show up for clinic or abandoning other clinical responsibilities. Although there is some variability in how the criteria for assigning a concern or deficiency are interpreted across the school's nine campuses, course or clerkship directors often engage the CD prior to submitting their assessment. Concerns are handled informally between the faculty member, the student, and the CD, whereas IDs involve a formal process that requires a "progress hearing" with SPC to determine whether the student will be able to remain in school or will be dismissed.

At the same time the concern or ID is registered, the student is notified of the action being taken. In the case of a concern, the CD is also alerted and information about the source of the concern is shared with him. The student is required to meet with the CD to discuss the concern and plan appropriate steps to deal with it. The CD then relays notes from the meeting to the course or clerkship director and there is ongoing informal communication about the student's progress in dealing with the concern. Importantly, competency concerns do not appear on the student's permanent record and thus do not play a role in the Dean's letter or any other formal record of the student's performance during medical school.

An ID automatically triggers a progress hearing before SPC. The committee consists of twenty-four faculty representing basic and clinical sciences from the nine campuses. Students called for a progress hearing are required to address the issues raised concerning their professionalism and present their explanation for the lapse(s) to the entire committee. In addition, the student is expected to propose a plan to address how he or she intends to deal with the deficiencies. A question period follows the student's presentation, after which the student is excused and the SPC votes on whether to dismiss the student or put him or her on probation with a required remediation.

In cases where SPC votes to dismiss a student, two options are available: the student may request another opportunity to present his or her case to the committee for a vote; if the second vote fails, he or she can make a final appeal to the Dean, who can choose to uphold or overturn SPCs decision.

As an alternative to dismissal, the committee can decide to place a student on academic probation and require successful remediation with the CD, who also sits on SPC. In this case, the student has an initial meeting with the CD, who evaluates the seriousness of the lapse, makes an educational assessment/diagnosis of the situation, and negotiates an agreed-upon remediation plan. Multiple face-to-face meetings may take place until the remediation is successfully completed. At that point, the CD reports back to SPC, which votes to accept or reject the recommendation to remove the student from academic probation and allow him or her to continue his or her studies, or to dismiss the student from medical school.

In the nine years that I was the professionalism CD, 105 students came before SPC for progress hearings. The majority of cases involved a single instance of a professionalism lapse that varied from falsifying documentation in a procedure log to signing others into lectures and other required activities. A smaller number of cases involved students who engaged in dishonest behavior, such as leaving the hospital cafeteria without paying for a meal. Similarly, there were a small number of more serious cases of dishonesty that involved cheating on exams or falsifying medical records. Finally, there was a handful of cases that involved accusations of cyberbullying and stalking. Of the students who came before SPC, six were deemed unremediable with a recommendation to dismiss from the medical school. Cheating was the most frequent lapse for which dismissal was recommended. The rest were successfully remediated in a process lasting from a month to one year.

Case study 1: Responding to a competency concern[12]

I received a phone call from a basic science course director at a regional campus asking whether I would meet with a second-year student who, in the course director's opinion, "was at risk for problems with professionalism." He described the student's behavior in the class he was teaching as inappropriate and childish, but not yet reaching the level of issuing an ID.

Prior to, and sometimes during, class the course director reported that the student would say things like, "This is the stupidest course I've ever taken," or, "The course instructor doesn't know what he's talking about half the time." While these comments weren't particularly hurtful personally, the director was concerned that the student's disruptive behavior was a risk factor that could potentially lead to his being sanctioned or even a losing privileges or his license to practice at some future point in his career. Since his own attempts to reach out to the student had been unsuccessful, he wondered if having the student meet with me would produce a different result. I readily agreed to meet with the student to discuss the concern.

Todd came into my office full of bravado and bluster. I first asked him if he knew why he was in my office. He explained that he had a conflict with the course director and that this meeting was his "punishment." He went on to say that the course director had it in for him because he had been born outside the United States and had been raised in New York City where things weren't quite so provincial. He then asserted that he really didn't care much about what others thought of him, especially the course director, as long as he got his work done and didn't fail any courses.

I listened carefully to Todd, internally testing my own experience of having grown up in New York City and now having lived in Indiana for twelve years, with what I was hearing. At the same time I was internally reviewing what type of remediation exercise might be effective for raising awareness about the importance of professional conduct for a student who was well-defended and might have impulse control challenges. Rather than give him a lecture on professionalism, which I thought would be unlikely to have any effect, I suggested that he read Maxine Papadakis' paper from the *New England Journal*[13] on the link between practicing physicians who come before state medical boards for unprofessional behavior and unprofessional behavior while in medical school, and that we talk again in the next two to three weeks. He reluctantly agreed.

Less than twenty-four hours after our encounter, I got an e-mail from Todd wondering if we could meet "sooner than two to three weeks." I happened to have an open hour in my schedule that day and replied, asking that he come in later that afternoon. Todd came into my office a different person. He looked exhausted and his eyes were red. I told him that I was surprised but glad to see him, to which he responded that he had read the Papadakis article the night before and had been "shocked" to discover that the article "described me to a 'T.'" Tears formed, and he shared his fear that there was real danger ahead for him if he continued on the path he was on. After a long pause, he wondered out loud what he could do to keep his dream of becoming a physician and serving society alive in the face of his self-defeating behaviors.

We talked about various options that might be available, including psychological counseling. Todd was eager to pursue this course of action and confessed that he had thought of it a year earlier but rejected the idea as "weak minded." After some discussion about what he thought would be helpful, we settled on a referral to a cognitive-behavioral therapist who works extensively with medical professionals. I had an opportunity to observe Todd in his third year in a small group narrative discussion that is held with students on their medicine rotation. At that point he seemed to have made a much better adjustment to his environment, those in authority, and his peers. The last contact I had with him was at graduation in 2011.

Analysis and comment

Three aspects of this case are worth commenting on: the opening gambit, the choice of remediation, and the result. In the literature on clinical interviewing, eliciting the patient's perspective before sharing one's own allows a clinician to adjust her or his response to the state of knowledge and point of view of the other rather than making inferences about what the patient does or does not know and understand.[14,15] In this case, eliciting the student's perspective at the beginning of the encounter allowed me to gather firsthand information about his perception about why the meeting was being held (as punishment). This opening gambit also allowed me to compare the student's point of view and contrast it with what I had heard from the course director (concern for the student's well-being).

The fact that the student felt as though he was being punished (persecuted) for his beliefs also provided important information about his point of view and likely responses to "suggestions," rather than a formal remediation program, i.e., the difference between a concern and an ID. Running through the various options that I had for dealing with a defensive student (similar to working with a "difficult" patient) I chose to simply present him with the best available data on what is known about professional behavior of medical students and their subsequent risk of coming before a state medical board for unprofessional behavior and let him draw his own conclusions. The motivational interviewing literature was helpful to me here in pointing out that rolling with resistance rather than confronting it is more likely to result in a change in behavior.[16] Evidence of the success of the choice of remediation approach and interviewing style is shown in the rapidity of the student's response, his openness to seeking help to change, and his successful graduation from medical school without further incident.

Case 2: A clear-cut case of cheating

Several years ago, the clerkship director for OB/GYN sent me a "heads up" about one of her students, Albert, who had been struggling during the last part of the rotation, for no obvious reason, and was observed to have cheated on the shelf exam. SPC had been notified that the student would be receiving an ID in professionalism and would be required to make an appearance before the committee. Parenthetically, cheating is known as a "capital offense" among many members of the SPC. It is a core precept of the school's honor code, and students who do cheat on exams have a high likelihood of being dismissed if cheating is confirmed. The clerkship director asked me to meet with the student to help him prepare for his SPC appearance. Before the meeting, I accessed his academic and competency transcript, which was excellent, and contained several course honors and no concerns or isolated deficiencies. I also reached out to the competency director for moral and ethical reasoning, with whom I had shared several cases, and asked her to be present at the pre-SPC meeting and partner in the remediation process.

Albert knocked on my office door, came in, sat down, crossed his arms over his chest, and was silent. My colleague and I asked if he knew why he was meeting with us and in a very matter-of-fact voice he said, "I cheated on the OB/GYN shelf exam," immediately averting his eyes and looking down, after which an uncomfortable silence ensued. We then shared with him that we had reviewed his excellent academic record and that in our experience when incidents like this occurred there was often something going on in the background that helped explain making poor choices like cheating. Was that the case here, we asked? Another uncomfortable silence ensued and then with great hesitation Albert told us about receiving the news of his fiancée's murder six days before the exam, and his feelings of helplessness and depression at being thousands of miles away. Through heaving sobs, he went on to describe his shame at what he had done and the consequences he would likely face after meeting with SPC.

After expressing our empathy for his loss and telling him that we understood how difficult it must have been for him to cope and to try maintain his studies, we encouraged Albert to share his story at his upcoming SPC hearing. He replied that he did not think it was possible to tell his story to twenty-four strangers and that he would sooner leave medical school than have to share his pain over what had happened. We reminded him that before this meeting we had been strangers and that he had been able, albeit with difficulty, to share his story with us. We offered to do a little bit of coaching and role playing about how to structure the presentation and an assured him that one of us would be there for support. In the end he agreed to present his story to SPC. Below is a fragment of the presentation he read to the committee.

> No matter how hard I tried, I couldn't get rid of the feelings of anger, rage, hopelessness, and guilt along with a constant tightness and chronic pain in my stomach . . . Toward the end of my OB/GYN clerkship, I found myself avoiding my work, avoiding people, and spending hours at a time in the restroom crying. I questioned everything that I ever believed in, including god. For the six days following that dreadful morning, I had little desire to do anything. As I sat for my OB/GYN exam, all I could do was think about her. Before I knew it, my time was running out and I made the poor decision of cheating on my exam, an action that in the past I had never even considered and for which I am deeply saddened and sorry.

After his presentation there were a few clarifying questions from members of the SPC who then voted unanimously to allow Albert to return to school after remediating his isolated deficiency. The remediation process included a recommendation for supportive counseling, doing library research and a paper on the problem of cheating in medical school, grief and mourning, writing letters of apology, and completing a personal reflection about the importance of asking for help and what his experience had taught him about professionalism and personal responsibility. Within minutes of receiving the news that he was going to be able to return to school after successful remediation Albert sent us an e-mail, part of which appears below:

> I had my meeting today and the SPC committee has voted to allow me to continue with school! I am extremely happy and feel as if a huge burden has been lifted off of my shoulders. I would just like to thank both of you from the bottom of my heart for everything that you have done for me. You made an extremely difficult situation a whole lot easier to handle. Your understanding and friendly nature was like a breath of fresh air and made me feel extremely comfortable. Once again, thank you for your help, and support. I am eagerly looking forward to this new beginning. Thank you once again!
> Sincerely,
> Albert

After his successful remediation and return to school, I did not hear from, or about, Albert for almost a year. It was his academic advisor who called me to discuss his "future." His advisor told me that Albert had expressed a strong desire to stay at IU for his residency but was convinced that it would not be possible given the cheating incident and the fact that it was on his transcript and in his Dean's letter. Together with my partner from the remediation process, and his advisor, we decided to contact the program director and offer our support for Albert's application. It turned out to be unnecessary as the program director had already decided to accept him based on his academic performance and a strong interview that included a detailed explanation of the incident, his remediation, and what he had learned about professionalism from the experience. Albert was accepted into the program where he performed with distinction. Below is a fragment of Albert's letter to me on Match Day, just after he learned he had been accepted to IU.

> From: Albert
>
> Dear Dr. Frankel:
>
> I hope all is well. As you probably know, "match day" was today and I was able to get my first choice . . . at IU! You have been kind and generous with your time, advice, suggestions and guidance and I wanted to make sure that I write and let you know the results of my match. Thank you so much for all of your help throughout. I could not have reached this point without your guidance.
>
> Albert

Albert is now in practice in the area, and has firmly established himself as a valued member of the medical community.

Analysis and comment

Like the first scenario, this case illustrates the importance of applying sound interviewing techniques, including empathy and support, to elicit the "narrative thread" of the events for which the student had been cited. In patient care, the narrative thread allows the interviewer to understand how clinical facts fit into the larger context of the patient's life world.[17–19] There are clear parallels in clinical medicine, for example, when patient behavior is viewed in isolation (e.g., a patient who fails to take her medication as prescribed) rather than in the context of their life situation (mother of four children who has no way to pay for the medication prescribed). The ability of the interviewer to explore the context of behavior in addition to the behavior itself is an important tool in clinical medicine that can be applied to remediation scenarios.

In interviewing the medical student before his meeting with SPC there was no question about the facts; the student himself said straightforwardly, "I cheated on the OB/GYN exam." However, his affect (flat) and nonverbal behavior (arms crossed over his chest, averted gaze, looking down and away, all signs of shame or embarrassment[20]) were clear signs that there was more to the narrative thread than his opening statement. It has been noted in the patient interviewing literature that clinician silence in the medical encounter, i.e., acting as a non-anxious presence, often builds trust and encourages the patient to continue speaking.[21–23] In this case, as uncomfortable as the silence might have felt, it revealed a story that was both compelling and heartbreaking. Although she was unsure why, it also matched the clerkship director's comment that the student had struggled in the rotation, about the same time that the student reported getting the news about his fiancée's murder. Once the student's "back story" emerged, my colleague and I both used empathy, active listening, and support—patient interviewing skills known to increase the likelihood of adherence to recommendations made in clinical care[24,25]—to help the student with the decision to tell his story to the SPC.

Evidence of the effectiveness of the pre-SPC meeting and remediation is demonstrated in having correctly read the student's non-verbal cues, using active listening and silence to create space for him to fill in the background of what happened around the time of the OB/GYN exam, corroboration of the timeline of events by the clerkship director, and genuine curiosity about the apparent disconnect between the student's previous performance and his behavior in the clerkship. In the broader ecology of his professional formation, the fact that the program director was willing to invest in a student who had suffered a serious professionalism lapse, his performance during residency, and subsequent success in practice also suggests that we made the right decisions in advocating for him.

Case 3: Double jeopardy and faculty responsibility

A third-year student on her medicine rotation received an ID in medicine for having cheated on the final exam. The clerkship director informed me that the student would be coming before SPC and asked whether I would meet with her to discuss the situation, which I agreed to do.

In response to my opening question about why she thought we were meeting, the student acknowledged that it was because she had cheated on the medicine exam. In providing background to her behavior she described herself as a perfectionist who always put pressure on herself to perform and said that she wanted to maintain her GPA and get honors in the rotation because she wanted to go into internal medicine. A few minutes into the meeting I asked her whether she had shared her situation with others; her parents, in particular. She replied tearfully that she had told her parents and her fiancé, and that these were two of the most difficult conversations she had ever had in her life. She went on to say that she was ashamed of her actions and really wanted to better understand her behavior. She explained that between the time of the incident and our meeting, she had sought psychological help and was seeing a psychiatrist twice a week, that she was getting spiritual counseling through her church, and had assembled an "accountability committee" with whom she met weekly. Finally, she said that she was gaining a lot of insight into the emotional triggers that made her anxious and feel inadequate under stress and was learning healthy ways of dealing with them.

All in all, it seemed as though the student's lapse had triggered a cascade of reflection and action that was helping her understand and deal with stress and the risks of her anxiety overriding her desire/ability to act professionally. In terms of preparing for her progress hearing with SPC, we discussed the need for transparency and honesty in taking responsibility for what had happened and the steps she was already taking to address her problems.

There was a two-month gap between the time that I met with her and her appearance before SPC. At her progress hearing the student presented a compelling account of all the steps she was taking, what she had learned about her response to stress, and healthy new habits and patterns that she was learning both in therapy and from her accountability committee. Toward the end of the meeting she put down her written statement, faced the committee and shared that as a first-year student there had been an incident in which she was observed to have briefly continued to work on an exam after the proctor had announced, "pencils down." She was asked to meet with the course director to talk about what had happened. The student said that she had apologized for her action and the course director told her that, "it wasn't a big deal," he wasn't going to report it, and that she should follow the proctor's instructions in the future. The student cited her sincere desire to get to the root of her "problem" and said that she wanted to be sure to leave no stone unturned in her quest for "the truth, the whole, and nothing but the truth."

When the student was excused from the hearing a long discussion ensued among the SPC committee members. Most agreed that she was taking all the right steps to better understand and deal with her triggers, and that she was thoughtful, sincere, and honest in her presentation. At the same time, several committee members argued that her admission of an earlier professionalism lapse, despite the fact that it was minor and was not officially documented or reported, constituted a "pattern" of behavior that was unacceptable for a medical student and recommended dismissal. By a narrow margin the committee voted for dismissal, which was upheld in the appeals process.

Analysis and comment

This case raises several important questions. First, in my meeting with the student, many of the recommended steps for an individual who acts unprofessionally were already being taken voluntarily (confronting the problem head-on, psychiatric and spiritual counseling, eagerness to explore and learn about the effect(s) of stress on behavior). In addition, the student had faced those she loved, her parents and fiancé, and had taken responsibility for her actions by informing them rather than hiding what she had done.

From the literature on patient interviewing a key question about high-risk behaviors that one might encounter in highly stigmatized areas such as marital infidelity, high-risk sex, and alcohol and drug use is to assess whether there is a pattern of behavior over time.[26] In retrospect, I realize that I failed to ask the student about whether she had experienced anything similar to the episode that occurred during the medicine rotation. Exploring the student's history in more depth might have revealed the previous incident and led to a conversation about the significance of the instructor's downplaying the incident and failing to take any action. It is, of course, speculation to believe that early detection and remediation would have prevented the student from additional cheating episodes, but it does seem likely that it would have helped her connect the dots and perhaps recognize that this behavior contributed to her dismissal from medical school.

A recently conducted national survey of medical schools' professionalism remediation approaches by Ziring and colleagues at Drexel College of Medicine found that the major reasons for failure to adequately address professionalism lapses were:

1. Faculty reluctance to report
2. Lack of faculty training
3. Unclear policies
4. Remediation ineffective

Factors cited for reluctance to report were: faculty discomfort in determining the seriousness of the problem, the increased workload reporting creates for them, concern about harming the student's future, the perceived minor nature of the witnessed lapse, and fear of repercussions.[27] These findings echo the theme of physicians protecting one another and refusing to fail students for unprofessional behavior.[28,29] As this case illustrates, my failure to elicit information about the frequency of the behavior in the pre-SPC meeting coupled with the reluctance of a faculty member to report the first instance of the student's questionable professional behavior essentially placed her in double jeopardy for telling the whole truth to the committee. Sadly, it wound up costing the student her opportunity to complete her medical training.

Conclusions

I began this chapter by noting that there has been exponential growth of interest in professionalism in the last two decades. This is a positive development as faculty, researchers, and administrators have sought to define and operationalize the concept. Consensus statements, such as the Charter on Medical Professionalism have seen simultaneous publication in multiple journals in the United States and elsewhere.[30] Many schools now have formal professionalism curricula and deans who support the importance of professional formation, as well as faculty who are responsible for maintaining professional standards and remediating students who have professionalism lapses.[31,32]

As interest in professionalism has grown, there has been corresponding interest in better understanding how different schools approach remediation and identifying best practices that can be translated into regional or national guidelines. The literature suggests, and my own experience confirms that, at present, each school is an island unto itself and that there is very little discussion and sharing about what constitutes an effective program of remediation from school to school. The need to systematically study this problem using evidence-based approaches has been identified and is gaining momentum.[10] One possible approach to identifying best practices in remediation would be to use the approach the Accreditation Council on Graduate Medical Education (ACGME) took in implementing its six-competency curriculum for all residents.[33] When they were introduced in 1999, ACGME "recommended" that all residents become competent in the competencies. It also asserted that evaluation of competencies was at a formative stage and that they would look to innovative strategies programs were developing and/or using to identify best practices. Four years later, in 2002, after having gathered systematic data on the most effective ways of evaluating the recommended competencies, the ACGME made successful evidence of achievement a requirement for graduation; not simply a recommended framework that was optional. The same strategy could be used to identify best remediation practices and over time use them to develop national guidelines with a common core of standards for evaluating the effectiveness of remediation processes.

Other approaches to reducing the fragmentation of knowledge about remediation in various medical schools might include collecting and reporting national data on the range of approaches schools take to deal with professionalism lapses. As well, offering skills-based faculty development and promoting a national dialogue about guidelines, opportunities, and challenges might help reduce the isolation of faculty charged with remediation. Finally, asking broader, deeper questions about medical school admissions practices and tools for identifying students who may be at risk for professionalism lapses could make the process of remediation more proactive than reactive.

The second theme of this chapter focused on the remediation encounter itself and methods drawn from evidence in the literature on patient interviewing. Faced with a paucity of practical information on how to conduct remediation encounters with students, I found that evidence-based patient-centered communication skills such as eliciting the patient's perspective, using empathy and support, reading non-verbal cues, and principles of motivational interviewing to be extremely helpful in establishing the narrative thread of events surrounding professional lapses. In addition, such techniques often provided the deeper understanding that could not be found or deduced from the student's file or the clerkship or course director's notes. I also found that comparing the story with the course or clerkship director's account allowed me to "triangulate" data from multiple sources that was helpful in confirming or disconfirming the student's account.[34] Using an evidence-based patient interviewing approach also permitted me to use a quality improvement framework to pinpoint errors in my own approach that could, and did, have significant consequences for at least one student.

The third theme was how we, as faculty, approach the remediation process. As the opening anecdote suggests, many faculty who do remediation work see it as difficult, challenging, and unrewarding, viewing it in much the same way as clinicians find working with difficult patients. Wendy Levinson, in a classic paper entitled "Mining for Gold," described how, after years of frustrating encounters, she found something to like about one of her most difficult patients when she explored the narrative thread of the patient's context, and how that understanding led to a positive transformation in their relationship and a shift in loyalty and trust.[35] The lesson here is that it is critically important to approach the remediation process with an open mind, to remember that all human beings have redeeming qualities, no matter how egregious their professional behavior may have been, and that context matters.[6] Whether helping a student regain his or her footing after a minor professionalism lapse or dealing with the possibility of dismissal after a major lapse, the goal, just as it is in patient care, should always be to find ways to be of service.

In closing, I suggest that we would do well to recall that the root word for remediation is *mederi*, which in Latin means "to heal." Together with the prefix *re*, which means "again," we arrive at a definition of remediation that focuses on strategies and approaches in working with students who have had professionalism lapses to heal again. As was true in the early days of the quality assurance movement, when the strategy was to weed out the bad apples, punish poor performance, and shame and humiliate those who didn't conform to quality standards, many now suggest that strategies focusing on intrinsic motivation, autonomy, and self-regulation are much more likely to succeed in producing high-quality results.[36,37] So, too, in approaching remediation encounters. If we re-frame the idea of punishing students for unprofessional behavior and instead treat it as an opportunity to help them heal (whether that means a student is dismissed or allowed to continue his or her medical education) we may find ourselves being more effective and more energized by the task, the process and the outcomes.

Acknowledgments

Many thanks go to Bud Baldwin, Frederic Hafferty, Thomas Inui, J. Harry (Bud) Isaacson, Deborah Ziring, and Liz Gaufberg for their careful reading of the manuscript and thoughtful suggestions for how to improve it.

References

1. Oxford English Dictionary (Compact Edition). Oxford: Oxford University Press; 1985.

2. Hafferty FW. Context (place) matters. Arch Pediatr Adolesc Med 2008; 162: 584–86.

3. Hafferty FW, Levinson D. Moving beyond nostalgia and motives: Towards a complexity science view of medical professionalism. Perspect Biol Med 2008; 51: 599–615.

4. Wynia MK, Papadakis MA, Sullivan WM, Hafferty FW. More than a list of values and desired behaviors: A foundational understanding of medical professionalism. Acad Med 2014; 89: 712–14.

5. Cruess RL, Cruess SR. Professionalism, laws and kings. Clin Invest Med 1997; 20: 407–13.

6. Lucey CR, Souba W. Perspective: The problem with the problem of professionalism. Acad Med 2010; 85: 1018–24.

7. Cruess RL, Cruess SR, Steinert Y, editors. Teaching Medical Professionalism. New York: Cambridge University Press; 2008.

8. Swiggart WH, Dewey CM, Hickson GB, et al. A plan for identification, treatment, and remediation of disruptive behaviors in physicians. Front Health Serv Manage 2009; 25: 3–11.

9. Hauer KE, Ciccone A, Henzel TR, et al. Remediation of the deficiencies of physicians across the continuum from medical school to practice: A thematic review of the literature. Acad Med 2009. 84: 1822–32.

10. Papadakis MA, Paauw DS, Hafferty FW, et al. Perspective: The education community must develop best practices informed by evidence-based research to remediate lapses of professionalism. Acad Med 2012; 87: 1694–98.

11. Buchanan AO, Stallworth J, Christy C, et al. Professionalism in practice:

Strategies for assessment, remediation, and promotion. Pediatrics 2012; 129: 407–9.

12. Frankel RM. Professionalism. In: Feldman M, Christensen J. Behavioral Medicine: A Guide for Clinical Practice. Third Edition. New York: McGraw-Hill; 2007: 424–30.

13. Papadakis MA, Teherani A, Banach MA, et al. Disciplinary action by medical boards and prior behavior in medical school. N Engl J Med 2005; 353: 2673–82.

14. Maynard DW. Perspective-display sequences in conversation. West J Speech Comm 1989; 53: 91–113.

15. Frankel, RM, Stein T, Krupat E. The Four Habits Approach to Effective Clinical Communication. Oakland (CA): Kaiser Permanente; 2003: 18.

16. Pollak KI, Childers JW, Arnold RM. Applying motivational interviewing techniques to palliative care communication. J Palliat Med 2011; 14: 587–92.

17. Haidet P, Paterniti D. "Building" a history rather than "taking" one: A perspective on information sharing during the medical interview. Arch Intern Med 2003; 163: 1134–40.

18. Charon R. Narrative Medicine: Honoring the Stories of Illness. New York: Oxford University Press; 2006.

19. Frankel RM, Quill T, McDaniel S, editors. The Biopsychosocial Approach: Past, Present, Future. Rochester (NY): University of Rochester Press; 2003.

20. Darwin C. The Expression of the Emotions in Man and Animals. London: John Murray; 1872.

21. Huby G. Interpreting silence, documenting experience: An anthropological approach to the study of health service users' experience with HIV/AIDS care in Lothian, Scotland. Soc Sci Med 1997; 44: 1149–60.

22. Fortin A. Dwamena FC, Frankel RM, Smith RC. Smith's Patient-Centered Interviewing: An Evidence-Based Method. Third Edition. New York: McGraw Hill; 2012.

23. Friedman EH. Generation to Generation: Family Process in Church and Synagogue. New York: Guilford Press; 1985.

24. Hojat, M, Louis DZ, Markham FW, et al. Physicians' empathy and clinical outcomes for diabetic patients. Acad Med 2011; 86: 359–64.

25. Milmoe S, Rosenthal R, Blane HT, et al. The doctor's voice: Postdictor of successful referral of alcoholic patients. J Abnorm Psychol 1967; 72: 78–84.

26. Smith DC, Hall JA, Jang M, Arndt S. Therapist adherence to a motivational-interviewing intervention improves treatment entry for substance-misusing adolescents with low problem perception. J Stud Alcohol Drugs 2009 70: 101–5.

27. Ziring D. Personal communication; 2014.

28. Wilkinson TJ, Tweed MJ, Egan TG, et al. Joining the dots: Conditional pass and programmatic assessment enhances recognition of problems with professionalism and factors hampering student progress. BMC Med Educ 2011;

11: 29.

29. Dudek NL, Marks MB, Regehr G. Failure to fail: The perspectives of clinical supervisors. Acad Med 2005; 80 (10 Suppl): S84–87.

30. ABIM Foundation. American Board of Internal Medicine; ACP-ASIM Foundation. American College of Physicians-American Society of Internal Medicine; European Federation of Internal Medicine. Medical professionalism in the new millennium: A physician charter. Ann Intern Med 2002; 136: 243–46.

31. Braddock CH III, Eckstrom E, Haidet P. The "new revolution" in medical education: Fostering professionalism and patient-centered communication in the contemporary environment. J Gen Intern Med 2004; 19 (5 Pt 2): 610–11.

32. Brater DC. Viewpoint: Infusing professionalism into a school of medicine: Perspectives from the dean. Acad Med 2007; 82: 1094–97.

33. Accreditation Council for Graduate Medical Education. Common Program Requirements. Chicago (IL): Accreditation Council for Graduate Medical Education; 2013. https://www.acgme.org/acgmeweb/Portals/0/PFAssets/ProgramRequirements/CPRs2013.pdf.

34. Inui TS, Sidle JE, Nyandiko WM, et al. "Triangulating" AMPATH: Demonstration of a multi-perspective strategic programme evaluation method. SAHARA J 2009; 6: 105–14.

35. Levinson W. Mining for gold. J Gen Intern Med 1993: 8: 172.

36. Deci EL, Ryan RM. Intrinsic Motivation and Self-Determination in Human Behavior. New York: Plenum Press; 1985.

37. Williams GC, Deci EL. The importance of supporting autonomy in medical education. Ann Intern Med 1998; 129: 303–08.

Summary

Chapter 10

Concluding Thoughts

George E. Thibault, MD

Today there is more and more interest in professionalism, and more discussion of it as something that we can and should teach. At the same time, there are more threats to professionalism and more examples that run counter to what we would think should be the professional behavior of physicians, other health professionals, and institutions.

So we are at this moment of tension. We actually know more about professionalism, and we have evolved from the point of thinking this is some kind of intrinsic moral quality to understanding that it is a set of behaviors that can be taught, can be learned, can be rewarded, and can be incented or dis-incented. But at the same time, we understand that the other changes that are going on, such as the commercialization of medicine, intense competition, resource constraints, and organizational changes that threaten autonomy all represent a continued threat to professionalism.

I suggest three ways I think we should be broadening the discussion for us as educators and leaders. First, the professionalism discussions should be about how we raise the consciousness and behavior of all students and trainees (not just those who need remediation). Second, we need to think about professionalism in the context of the organizations in which we all function and how these organizations can have positive or negative influences on professional behavior. And third, we should be thinking about an inter-professional professionalism that involves the other health professions that are our partners in caring and teaching.

I want to offer a definition of professionalism provided by U.S. Supreme Court Judge Louis Brandeis a century ago. Brandeis identified three characteristics of the learned professions. First, a learned profession is in possession of a special set of knowledge and skills that it is responsible for mastering, for improving, and for passing on to the next generation. Second, a learned profession puts others' interests ahead of its own. Third, a learned profession is self-regulating.

This has been a helpful framework for me, and I think I can link most of the behaviors we are seeking to teach and measure to these three principles. Reductionism to the particular behaviors is important to define a curriculum and an assessment system, but I believe it is important that this be done within a higher framework.

There are two important parts to realizing that professionalism does not happen in a vacuum: one has to do with the entire educational environment and the second has to do with the relationship between education and health care delivery.

Structures to help us monitor and correct behaviors will not mean anything if they are not consistent with everything else that we say and do from day one on. It does matter what we teach in the curriculum, and it does matter how we structure the curriculum. But it also does matter how we form relationships between faculty and students and how we set examples and model behaviors. Talk about the resistance to "forward feedback" reminds me of how broken our system is. Because we are so worried that students and faculty will have nothing other than very casual encounters, we don't believe that constructive feedback will or can be given. If we do not do something about that, then we are not being consistent when we say we are going to put a system in place to remediate unprofessional behavior. The whole structure and environment have to support what it is we want to accomplish. Understanding there are a lot of impediments, we have a responsibility to deal with the things that are getting in the way of our goals. Unless we do that, then the best measurement and remediation system in the world is not going to work. We have to show that we really care, and that we are fixing things that don't work in our educational system. We must be consistent in how we set up our whole educational process so that it fosters continuity of relationships and models the behaviors we want our students to learn.

The second part of this not occurring in a vacuum is that the medical school and the medical students are part of a larger health care system. While the medical school in most instances does not control the rest of that system, it must interact with it. We have a responsibility to our students and to our profession to do a better job at building the bridges between the educational system and the delivery system. We will not be successful in our professionalism goals unless we do that. That is hard work, and it is frustrating at times. We often feel like we live in different worlds and cultures, but we have got to bridge that gap or we are not going to succeed. We need to articulate how the educational goals connect with the rest of the health care system. We need to make clear how the rest of the health care system shares the responsibility for creating the ideal educational environment for our next generation of health professionals. We will not succeed unless we build those bridges with others. Education needs to be informed by the needs of the public and the changing delivery system; and the changing delivery system must embrace and incorporate the educational mission.

The last observation I would make is that this is about culture change. Some have compared professionalism to the quality and patient safety movement. Yes, it is a professional responsibility not to harm patients and to constantly improve, but professionalism is more than that. It is also a professional responsibility to work with and respect other health professionals and acknowledge when they know more than we do. It also is a professional responsibility to assure one's own competency and the competency of the next generation of our profession. It also is our professional responsibility to work with other health professions in setting the standards for those competencies. And we do all of this because we exist as professionals to serve the public, and we earn our special privileges only if we do that. So we are back to the Brandeis definition of professionalism, but with a realization that this professionalism is not a solo activity. To accomplish it (and teach it) we need to effect a culture change in which we break down the silos between the professions and function in a non-hierarchical way; we must become truly patient-centered rather than profession-centric; we must focus on the needs of the community in designing both education and care; and we must create the kind of caring and collaborative environment in which our students see professionalism modeled and receive the constructive feedback they deserve.

Chapter 11

Improving Professionalism in Medicine: What Have We Learned?

Sheryl A. Pfeil, MD

The preceding chapters, authored by diverse experts in medical professionalism, bring valuable information and underscore an important challenge facing our profession: How do we hold ourselves to the highest standards of professional conduct under all circumstances? And what do we do—what *should* we do—when we fall short?

George Thibault reminds us, in his concluding remarks following the 2013 AΩA summit, that professionalism is neither an intrinsic moral quality nor a set of attributes and beliefs, but a set of behaviors that can be taught, learned, rewarded, incentivized, and disincentivized (see Chapter 10). As such, professionalism encompasses the standards of conduct and the observable behaviors that stem from our underlying belief system. Self-regulation is fundamental to any profession, but particularly so to medicine, built as it is on the covenant of trust the profession has with patients and society.

Professionalism is a core competency for all physicians. All medical professionals, whether established or newly entering the profession, need to embrace the values of medical professionalism and demonstrate the aptitude and commitment to behave professionally. It is true that many things in the day-to-day world of health care can stress the behavior of even the most professional physicians. These may include system pressures such as resource constraints, productivity and efficiency expectations, and organizational challenges. There may be value conflicts, patient conflicts, Maslow conflicts. Furthermore, the rules of professionalism are contextual, and the professional response to complex situations may be nuanced (see Chapter 1). But these acknowledged complexities do not diminish the imperative for us, as a profession, to hold ourselves accountable for sustaining professionalism.

If ever there were a case for lifelong learning, sustaining professionalism would be it. Even the most experienced practitioner must be continuously self-vigilant as new challenges, new systems, and new expectations arise. We need to consciously engage in and model professional behaviors in our interactions with patients, team members, and the health system. Medical students and other learners are particularly vulnerable—they learn what they see and experience in the "hidden curriculum." When those of us who should be positive role models demonstrate disruptive behaviors such as intimidation, making disparaging remarks about patients or other team members, or specialty bashing, and—worse yet—when we collectively and systematically tolerate these behaviors, we threaten our culture of professionalism and send a dangerous message to learners (see Chapter 1). But when we model professional behaviors, eschew cronyism, and embrace a culture of respect and collegiality, we create a positive professional culture that "raises all boats."

Professionalism lapses and remediation: Does one size fit all?

A critical component of professionalism is a commitment to self and group regulation and accountability. We need to respond or intervene when a lapse is identified. We have been made keenly aware of the importance of identifying professionalism shortcomings among students by Papadakis et al., who in a 2004 report linked professionalism lapses in medical school to future disciplinary action by a medical licensing board.[1,2] There is a growing understanding that the formation of professional identity is a developmental and dynamic process; learners will inevitably make mistakes and will require guidance or remediation before becoming full professionals. But remediation has little value unless it predictably leads to improvement, and little is known about what the best practices are or should be. What is the right thing to do? How should we assess improvement? How long should we follow student progress? Should information about student lapses feed forward to future evaluators?

In response to these types of questions, Ziring et al. surveyed medical schools in the United States and Canada to learn about their policies and procedures for identifying and remediating professionalism lapses among students (see Chapter 3). Most schools have written policies and procedures regarding medical student professionalism lapses, including descriptions of expectations, mechanisms for reporting, and potential consequences. Using the Papadakis four-category behavioral classification of professionalism lapses (see Chapter 1), the most common reported categories of professionalism lapses were: 1) lapses in responsibility (e.g., late or absent for assigned responsibilities, missing deadlines, unreliable); followed by 2) lapses related to the health care environment (e.g., testing irregularities such as cheating or plagiarism, falsifying data or not being respectful to members of the health care team); and 3) lapses related to diminished capacity for self-improvement (e.g., arrogant, hostile, or defensive behavior); with only a few schools identifying frequent concerns in the domain of 4) lapses around impaired relationships with patients (e.g., poor rapport, being insensitive to patients' needs).

Some of the remediation strategies included mandated mental health evaluation/treatment, completion of a professionalism assignment such as directed reading and reflective writing, assigning a professionalism mentor, stress/anger management, and repeating part or all of a course. Some schools issued a behavioral or remediation "contract." Some schools took more of a punitive stance and others took a more developmental approach. Regardless of the strategy, the criteria for successful remediation were not well defined.

The feeding forward of information about a student's lapses to the next clerkship or assignment was also inconsistent, and sometimes depended on the stage of training and type of lapse. While forward feeding was sometimes used to track performance and guide students, there was also concern about its potential to create bias.

When asked what was working well, schools identified themes such as catching minor offenses early, emphasizing professionalism school-wide, focusing on helping rather than punishing students, and assuring transparency and communication of expectations and consequences. The major weaknesses included reluctance to report by both faculty and students, the lack of faculty training, unclear policies, and ineffectiveness of remediation strategies (see Chapter 3).

Lucey adds additional insight about why faculty who witness unprofessional behavior may be reluctant to report it. She describes the behaviors of denial (it wasn't unprofessional), discounting (it was unprofessional but it was warranted), or distancing (it was unprofessional but let's just move on).[3] Lucey also adds that failing to correct a professionalism lapse may be because faculty lack confidence in their ability to intervene successfully or because they are concerned that a report to an authority could result in sanctions disproportionate to the severity of the witnessed behavior (see Chapter 2).

In Frankel's detailed description of the tiered professionalism competency program at Indiana University School of Medicine, he describes a two-pathway approach to managing professionalism lapses (see Chapter 9). Course directors or faculty members may enter a "competency concern" or "isolated deficiency." Competency concerns are handled informally between the faculty member, the student, and the Competency Director; they do not appear on the student's permanent record and do not play a role in the MSPE (Dean's letter). On the other hand, isolated deficiencies automatically trigger a progress hearing before the Student Promotions Committee. This two-pathway approach allows consideration of the severity of the lapse, and provides a mechanism for reporting with limited adverse consequences when the infraction is less serious.

Across the board, the considerations that are most often cited as relevant in addressing and remediating professionalism lapses include the gradation or severity of the offense, whether there is a pattern of professionalism lapses (recidivism), and the stage of the learner. While some institutions have separate processes for addressing medical student and physician professionalism lapses, other institutions assume a more holistic, medical center–wide or even interprofessional approach. Indeed, as the ways that we provide health care and are reimbursed for doing so change, it will be imperative to address the professionalism competencies of multidisciplinary and interprofessional groups and the individuals working within them. Payment models will increasingly focus on care coordination, requiring hospitals and physician providers to work together. Reimbursement will be increasingly focused on value, quality, and outcomes that necessitate interdisciplinary care collaboration and resource sharing. As we move to more value-driven, accountable care, the ways that we deliver care and, consequently, our professional behavior, will become more interdisciplinary, more interprofessional, and more interconnected. Professional behaviors will be demonstrated and judged in new dimensions and contexts, across the continuum of learning stages and across the spectrum of health provider roles and relationships.

What is working?

As we seek to acknowledge, prevent, and remedy the problems of professionalism within medicine, it is helpful to look at "best practices" in health care systems nationwide. What is working, and why? Is anything working? If so, is it generalizable? Hickson and Cooper in Chapter 7 described the Vanderbilt approach to promoting professionalism. This exemplar model was developed with the precepts that there must be leadership commitment to hold all members of the group accountable for professional behavior, as well as support by people, processes, and technology to provide an infrastructure to address lapses in professionalism. Core principles of the Vanderbilt model include fairness and justice, "certainty" of data, a commitment to provide individuals the opportunity through feedback to develop personal insight, and a goal of restoration, allowing the individual to regain the honor of being a professional. A hallmark of the Vanderbilt model is the professional accountability pyramid. Beginning at the lowest tier, a single unprofessional incident is addressed by an informal, "cup of coffee" intervention, an apparent pattern of unprofessional behavior is addressed by a level 1 "awareness" intervention, a persistent pattern necessitates a level 2 "guided" intervention and refractory unprofessional behavior may lead to disciplinary action. Standards of practice and conduct are enforced consistently and equitably, regardless of the individual's stature or value to the organization, and there is clear protection of the reporter from retaliation.

As described by Shapiro in Chapter 5, the Brigham and Women's Hospital Center for Professionalism and Peer Support (CPPS) was created to support and encourage a culture of accountability, trust, and mutual respect in which physicians feel supported and valued. When a concern is brought forth, the CPPS staff first meets with the reporter, then speaks with others to gather multisource data before bringing the concern to the individual's supervisory physician. The center staff and supervisory physician meet with the focus person to give frame-based feedback. The goal is to focus on the behavior, explain that the behavior needs to stop, and describe the expected behavior going forward, with the intent of motivating the individual to change his or her behavior. Does the process work? Since 2009, of 242 individual physicians about whom concerns were raised and 10 instances of team dysfunction, there has been retraction (by departure or demotion) of only 31 physicians. CPPS acknowledges the need for unwavering institutional support of the process. They also recognize that people perform best in a supportive environment and have developed various peer support programs to accomplish this goal.

As Saavedra reports in Chapter 6, the University of Texas Medical Branch (UTMB) has developed a mix of programs aimed at understanding, influencing, promoting, and monitoring an enterprise-wide culture of interprofessional professionalism. UTMB considers professionalism a standard of conduct and a strategic objective. This multidisciplinary approach is led by a Professionalism Committee. The UTMB Professionalism Charter extends to all faculty, staff, and students, and its mandate is "to hold every member of the UTMB community accountable for acting with integrity, compassion and respect towards one another and those we serve." The Charter is comprised of thirteen commitments that address such specifics as professional competence, honesty, conflicts of interest, and access to health care. Students have developed an honor pledge shared by students in all four schools, and UTMB has created a number of proactive programs to support these commitments, including interprofessional education courses, programs to recognize exemplary models of professional behavior, and a professionalism summit. To maintain the professional education climate, the school has an online mechanism for students to report unprofessional behavior or mistreatment. Concerns about student professionalism lapses are addressed by an Early Concern Note (ECN), an informal intervention separate from the student's academic record that remains confidential between the student and the associate dean unless a student receives three or more ECNs during matriculation. Does this program work? A laudable feature of the UTMB program is that a series of student, employee, and patient surveys are used to promote and measure the effectiveness of the program over time and across multiple stakeholders. UTMB reports the survey data and uses the results for constructive improvement. The UTMB program is an example of a system-wide approach to address and sustain health care professionalism by a culture of shared values and interdisciplinary collaboration.

The Vanderbilt, Brigham and Women's, and UTMB models represent examples of well-established programs in professionalism monitoring and remediation. Yet for these programs and others, there is limited evidence, beyond feasibility, of their success. Outcome studies over the long term after remediation remain critical. Are we effecting long-term behavior change on the part of individuals, and are we positively influencing systems to facilitate better care? Is there an eventual payoff for the public from the effort, cost, and effect on clinicians of these strategies? These are the critical questions that beg for future outcome analyses.

Bringing other models to bear on the problem of professionalism

Beyond the exemplars described above, what other system models might help us effectively address professionalism shortcomings? Do we have evaluative processes and change models used in other contexts that might be useful in improving medical professionalism and professional behaviors?

In 2008, the Joint Commission issued a sentinel event alert statement that underscored the direct relationship between unprofessional behavior and quality of patient care:

> Intimidating and disruptive behaviors can foster medical errors, contribute to poor patient satisfaction and to preventable adverse outcomes, increase the cost of care, and cause qualified clinicians, administrators and managers to seek new positions in more professional environments. Safety and quality of patient care is dependent on teamwork, communication, and a collaborative work environment. To assure quality and to promote a culture of safety, health care organizations must address the problem of behaviors that threaten the performance of the health care team.[4]

This direct connection between behaviors and patient outcomes begs the question of whether professionalism lapses should be considered analogous to—or a form of—medical error.

In Chapter 2 of this monograph, Lucey frames the challenge of sustaining professionalism as a complex adaptive problem, and she describes the similarities between medical errors and professionalism lapses, noting that at times, "those who we otherwise consider to be good physicians . . . commit professionalism lapses [resulting from] a temporary mismatch between the individual's knowledge, judgment, or skill and the complexity of the situation in which they find themselves."[p14] Like medical errors, professionalism lapses vary in severity and occur predictably (e.g., when individuals are stressed, the situations are highly charged, and controversy is present). Lucey points out that the systems in which we care for patients and educate our learners can either help us sustain our professional values and behaviors or render us susceptible to failure. Acknowledging the role of the system and the environment allows us to understand the complexity of professionalism lapses and to employ a root cause analysis model to devise strategies to help us address or prevent lapses. Lucey also explores the concept of "latent errors"—decisions about how health care systems are run that may predispose to "latent lapses"—when the system fails to protect the vulnerable patient from the fallible physician. She challenges us to view professionalism not as a dichotomous character trait but as a complex and renewable competency, and to approach professionalism from the perspective that even those most deeply committed to practicing the values of professionalism will sometimes be challenged by circumstances and environments that are trying and arduous. Lucey advocates teaching skills of "professionalism resiliency," shaping health care delivery systems to support a culture of professionalism, and championing positive examples.

If we indeed view professionalism as a complex multidimensional competency and a developmental process, what lessons can we bring from other competency-based education, such as the development of clinical skills? It is clear that in the domain of professionalism competency we must develop similarly robust ways to identify low performers, accurately describe the deficits, design a remediation program, and then measure the outcomes. Because professionalism competency is vital for both learners and the learners' future patients, Chang in Chapter 8 emphasizes the importance of early identification of deficits and the relevance of comparing the learner's performance with expected milestones using objective measures, just as would routinely be done for medical knowledge and clinical skills.

Finally, the measurement of outcomes after remediation remains a challenging task in every domain, but especially in professionalism, as Chang notes. Do we aim to change the learner's attitude, behavior, or both? How do we systematically document performance, and what opportunities do we have for reassessment other than absence of negative reports? What if the improvement is not consistent across settings or over time? These and other questions remind us of what still needs to be learned about remediation.

Concluding remarks

So what is the take home message? We have heard from experts who represent widespread geographic and system diversity and who bring perspectives about the continuum from student learner to senior faculty. How do we get to where we want to be? How do we achieve and sustain the highest level of professionalism in all of our systems for the benefit and protection of patients, learners, and practitioners alike? How do we remain ready to meet the next new challenge in professionalism and continue to reach for innovative approaches? The models that have been presented focus not just on the individual, but on the culture and systems that underlie our performance within a complex environment.

When we consider the remediation of professionalism—or perhaps more euphemistically the improvement of professionalism—five principles help frame our call to action:

1. Professional identity formation and professionalism competency, while inextricable, are not the same. Professional identity is the self or being that develops as the "characteristics, values, and norms of the medical profession are internalized, resulting in an individual thinking, acting and feeling like a physician."[5] Professionalism, on the other hand, is a behavior that is observable, measureable, and—by its nature—modifiable. Professionalism is a complex competency[6] that is contextual, dynamic, and both individual and shared. Those who observe and evaluate professionalism include attending physicians, patients, co-workers, and students. Because feedback about professionalism comes from multiple sources and by varied means, ranging from incident reports to formal evaluations, we need a better system to collect and synthesize this information so that we can intervene most effectively.

2. We need to hold individuals accountable for their behavior. When professional lapses occur, they negatively affect patients, colleagues, students, and other members of the health care team. Worse yet, students learn what they see, and unprofessional behavior that is tolerated, ignored, or allowed to continue is likely to be emulated. Standards of professionalism need to be upheld unconditionally regardless of an individual's seniority or institutional stature. And to respond appropriately as observers, we need both to be able to recognize lapses in professionalism when we see and experience them and to have the resources and systems in place to respond appropriately. Interventions need to be step-wise and specific to the lapse.

3. We need to hold systems accountable. Health care systems substantially influence the behavior of physicians and others who practice within them and can thus directly impact patients, employees, and the larger community. We need to recognize and raise awareness of the

environmental barriers—resource constraints, productivity pressures, competing expectations, conflicting goals, and other system pressures—that make it more difficult to align our behavior with our professional standards. And we need to hold health care organizations accountable for competencies of service, respect, fairness, integrity, accountability, and mindfulness.[7]

4. Remediation of professionalism lapses needs to be foremost formative rather than punitive. Unprofessional behaviors in well-intentioned physicians often occur when they lack the knowledge, skills, adaptability, self-awareness, or personal resources to manage the challenges they face. We have an obligation to help physicians understand how their unprofessional behaviors are perceived and how they affect patients and the health care team, as well as to explore root causes and develop plans to prevent future lapses. We can further support change by providing ongoing feedback and reinforcement of positive behaviors.

5. We need to study the outcomes of what we are doing. This, more than anything, is our imperative. We need to evaluate whether our interventions are effective over the long term. What strategies are best for each learner level, type of lapse, or circumstance? The task of improving professionalism is hard work, and we need to gather information to guide and refine our efforts.

The secret to achieving our goal of improving professionalism lies in understanding its complexity and being willing to accept that professionalism is a universal, dynamic, renewable, and contextual competency. We need to tackle this head on, bringing our combined energies, ingenuity, creativity, and focus to bear on this issue. There is no greater threat to our profession than our own professionalism, and no greater opportunity to sustain the worth of what we do. Assuring professionalism in the way we deliver health care is the single most important call to action, and one at which we must succeed if we are to maintain the sacrosanct covenant of public trust and demonstrate universally that we can live up to the promises and expectations of competency and ethical values—that we are indeed "worthy to serve the suffering."

References

1. Papadakis MA, Hodgson CS, Teherani A, Kohatsu ND. Unprofessional behavior in medical school is associated with subsequent disciplinary action by a state medical board. Acad Med 2004; 79: 244–49.

2. Papadakis MA, Teherani A, Banach MA, et al. Disciplinary action by medical boards and prior behavior in medical school. N Engl J Med 2005; 353: 2673–82.

3. Mizrahi T. Managing medical mistakes: Ideology, insularity and

accountability among internists-in-training. Soc Sci Med 1984; 19: 135–46.

4. Joint Commission on Accreditation of Health Care Organizations. Sentinel Event Alert 40: Behaviors that Undermine a Culture of Safety. Oakbrook Terrace (IL): Joint Commission on Accreditation of Health Care Organizations 2008 Jul 9; 40. http://www.jointcommission.org/assets/1/18/SEA_40.PDF.

5. Cruess RL, Cruess SR, Boudreau JD, et al. Reframing medical education to support professional identity formation. Acad Med 2014; 89: 1446–51.

6. ABIM Foundation, American Board of Internal Medicine; ACP-ASIM Foundation, American College of Physicians-American Society of Internal Medicine; European Federation of Internal Medicine. Medical professionalism in the new millennium: a physician charter. Ann Intern Med 2002; 136: 243–46.

7. Egener B, McDonald W, Rosof B, Gullen D. Perspective: Organizational professionalism: Relevant competencies and behaviors. Acad Med 2012; 87: 668–74.